Treasures of the
LOUVRE

Treasures of the
LOUVRE

Maria Costantino

BISON GROUP

First published in 1992 by
Bison Books Ltd
Kimbolton House
117A Fulham Road
London SW3 6RL

Copyright © 1992 Bison Books Ltd

ISBN 0-86124-950-X

Printed in Hong Kong

Page 1 I M Pei's controversial pyramid,
constructed in the Louvre courtyard in 1986–87
and giving access to a vast underground
reception area.

Page 2 Jean Clouet: *Portrait of King Francis 1,*
c. 1535. The first major building program in the
development of the Louvre as it appears today
was initiated by the Renaissance monarch
Francis I.

Right Gilgamesh or *The Propitiatory Genius of a
Hero,* late eighth century BC. The Louvre's
Middle Eastern holdings were greatly extended
as a result of the conquests of Napoleon
Bonaparte.

Contents

Introduction

The Louvre was not the first public museum, being preceeded by the Ashmolean Museum in Oxford, the Vatican Museum in Rome, the British Museum in London and in America by the Charleston Museum. It is nonetheless not only a great international collection, but the largest national gallery in the world, while the building itself is a record of over 800 years of French history and culture.

It is possible that there was a Frankish tower or fortified camp on the site of the Louvre at the end of the fifth century AD, during the time of Clovis I's seige of the remaining Gallo-Roman forces in Paris, since the name 'Louvre' itself may be derived from the Frankish *louver*, meaning a fortified chateau. Alternatively the origin of the name may be derived from *louveterie*, the headquarters of the wolf hunt, or even from the name of a leper colony. The earliest known structure on the present site was a medieval fortress begun in about 1190 by King Philip Augustus. This Louvre, of which traces can still be seen, was built outside the city walls of Paris and consisted of a large circular tower and courtyard surrounded by deep moats. To the west and south of

the courtyard were battlements, while to the north and east stood crenellated façades. The whole structure, which stood in the southwest quarter of the present court of the Old Louvre, was used mainly as a fortress, arsenal and treasure house. While prisoners languished in the dungeons, the upper rooms of the Louvre served as strongholds containing royal jewels, sacred relics, devotional objects, illuminated manuscripts and ceremonial armor.

Despite its small size – the courtyard measured only some 160 by 200 feet compared with the present Louvre which, with the Tuileries gardens, covers some 45 acres – the Louvre became a symbol of enduring strength, and its career as a center of wealth and splendor had begun. In the thirteenth century it functioned as a royal retreat, in which were hosted banquets, tournaments and state occasions. Where the present Gallery of the Caryatids is located, Louis IX (1214-70), commonly called Saint Louis, used an enlarged room to administer justice. By the 1350s, the Louvre's military function as a fortress had ended. A group of rebellious merchants led by Etienne Marcel

Left A reconstruction of the Louvre, part fortress, part royal residence, as it was at the time of Philip Augustus.

Above The Louvre as depicted by a fifteenth-century Flemish painter in the *Reredos of the Paris Parlement.*

gained possession of the Louvre and subsequently enclosed the building with new extensions to the city walls.

During the reign of Charles V (1338–80), the Louvre became a part-time royal residence and in 1365 an army of architects, masons and artists was employed to modernize the building. Extended to the north and east by the addition of two new wings to replace the original crenellated façades, the donjon or keep was now entirely surrounded by buildings. A contemporary manuscript illumination from the *Tres Riches Heures* of the Duc du Berry and a Flemish painting *Reredos of the Paris Parlement* both show a castle that is quadrilateral in shape, flanked by double towers and roofed in glazed tiles. In addition to the extensions to the building, Charles' library, started 100 years earlier by his ancestor Louis IX, was enlarged to become the nucleus of the present Bibliothèque Nationale.

Despite the elegant extensions, however, Charles was still obliged to sleep in a garret when he entertained the King of Bohemia and his entourage in 1377. The cramped spaces of the Louvre made it difficult for succeeding kings to use the building as a residence and in 1415, after the defeat of the French under Charles VI (1368-1422) at Agincourt, the Louvre was overrun by the English and many of its treasures plundered. For nearly 150 years the Louvre was neglected, once more reverting to a prison and arsenal while its picturesque outbuildings and gardens fell into decay and ruin.

The accession of Francis I (1494-1547) to the throne of France in 1515 marked the end of the Louvre's role as a medieval fortress and the first steps toward its present function as treasure house. By 1527, Francis had ordered the demolition of the old tower of the Louvre, while in the following year he commissioned the mason Gilles Le Breton to construct a royal palace at Fontainebleau. It was here that Francis began his collection of paintings which was to form the nucleus of the national collection. Having persuaded Leonardo da Vinci to come to France, Francis installed the Florentine painter in a house at Cloux near Amboise. Although by this time Leonardo's hand was paralyzed and he could do little painting, he had brought with him to France three paintings which the king appears to have purchased: *St. John the Baptist, The Virgin and*

Left Leonardo da Vinci: *John the Baptist*. Leonardo was persuaded by King Francis 1 to take up residence in France toward the end of his life. Although too enfeebled to paint, he brought a number of paintings, including this one, with him. Popular legend has it that he died in the king's arms.

Right The Square Court, begun in 1546 by Pierre Lescot on the orders of Francis 1, set a new standard in classicizing Renaissance decoration for French architecture.

Child with Saint Anne and *La Giaconda* (or *Mona Lisa*). Further paintings were also sent to Francis as diplomatic gifts, including two by Raphael, *The Holy Family* and *St Michael*, given to the king by Lorenzo II de' Medici on behalf of Pope Leo X. Strangely, the king's paintings were not deposited in the galleries of the state apartments at Fontainebleau, but placed in either the chapel or the 'Chambres de Bains,' which were bathing and retiring rooms.

On August 2nd, 1546, Francis commissioned Pierre Lescot, one of the greatest architects of the sixteenth century, to erect a new Louvre building on the site of Philip Augustus's fortress, although the king's collection was to remain at Fontainebleau until the middle of the seventeenth century. When Francis died in August 1547, his successor Henry II (1519-59) continued and extended the building program under Lescot, and it became the first French example of the classicizing architectural tradition established by Filippo Brunelleschi in the early fifteenth century in Renaissance Florence. Lescot's elegant façade, decorated with sculptures by Jean Goujon, had replaced the west wing of the old chateau by 1548. In the original design, the

new building (now the west wing of the Cour Carrée) was to be flanked on either side by two small galleries. During the 1550s this plan was radically enlarged to incorporate a court enclosed by blocks double the length of Lescot's wing, although the new scheme was not executed until the following century. The king's apartments were situated in another new building, the 'Pavillon du Roi,' built on the site of what is now the 'Salle des Sept Cheminées.'

Building work was continued not only by Henry but by his widow, Catherine de' Medici, as regent for the infant Charles IX (1550-74). In 1564, Catherine commissioned her favorite architect Philibert de l'Orme, an even more innovatory figure than Lescot, to build for her a country residence conveniently close to the Louvre on a spot known as the Tuileries. The following year she devised a new scheme, based on Vasari's plans to link the Uffizi Gallery and the Pitti Palace in Florence by means of a gallery running along the River Arno. The Paris scheme was to link the Louvre and the Tuileries by a 'Grande Galerie,' part of which was to follow the line of Charles V's city walls alongside the River Seine. This gallery was to connect at right angles with the Pavillon du Roi by means of a new 'Petite Galerie.' Catherine succeeded in building only this little gallery. The Grande Galerie scheme was finally carried out by Henri IV (1533-1610) between 1595 and 1610, designed by Louis Métezeau and Jacques Androuet du Cerceau the Younger. Beneath the 480 yards of the Grande Galerie were placed numerous artists' studios and lodgings, while the gallery itself was simply a long empty hall. The Petite Galerie was full of royal portraits; portraits of the kings of France were arranged down one side, with their queens displayed between the windows on the opposite wall. Known as the 'Galerie des Rois,' the Petite Galerie was a royal 'family tree' in pictures.

On the second floor of the Pavillon du Roi was a 'Cabinet des Armes,' while above, on the third floor, was the Grand Cabinet where Henri IV held audiences. In this room were contained the precious objects and regal paraphernalia which the kings bequeathed to their heirs. Louis XIII (1601-43), Henry IV's son, was especially fond of this room and often sought peace and refuge there. Louis continued the building program by announcing that construction work on the Louvre was to be resumed. In 1624 the first stone was laid and a commemorative medal struck to mark the occasion. Under the direction of the architect Jacques Lemercier,

the enclosing of the Cour Carrée on four sides, the plan conceived at the time of Henri II, was begun. Lemercier doubled the size of Lescot's wing, constructing the Pavillon de l'Horloge, decorated with caryatids, as a new centerpiece, and laid the foundations for the north-west corner pavilion of the north wing bordering the rue de Rivoli.

It was now the turn of the Grande Galerie, left empty at the end of Henri IV's reign, to be suitably decorated. In 1641, advised by his Directeur des Bâtiments (Superintendent of Buildings), Sublet de Noyers, Louis summoned the painter Nicolas Poussin from Rome. He set to work preparing cartoons for a great decorative scheme of paintings and stucco work for the vaulted ceiling, representing the life of Hercules. This was never realized, however, and the cartoons are now in the Cabinet des Dessins in the Louvre. Caught up in court intrigues and constantly battling with Lemercier, Poussin finally fled back to Rome.

While Louis XIII added greatly to the fabric of the Louvre, he added very little to the royal collections. Patronage on a magnificent scale, and often with state funds, was carried out by Cardinal Richelieu, chief minister in France 1624-42, and the works of art he amassed for his own pleasure and benefit filled his Paris residence, the Palais Royal and his two châteaux at

Left This nineteenth-century engraving shows the eastern courtyard of the Louvre, with the seventeenth-century facade known as the Colonnade in the foreground. Lemercier's three-story centerpiece, the Pavillon de l'Horloge, dominates the Cour Carrée, while behind it lie the Tuileries palace and gardens.

Right Jacques Lemercier began to realize the fifteenth-century plan to enclose the Cour Carrée in 1624, by doubling the size of Lescot's wing and creating the Pavillon de l'Horloge as a linking motif.

Rueil and Poitou. Richelieu's collection included works by Perugino, Mantegna, Leonardo, the Carracci brothers, Veronese and Poussin. The cardinal bequeathed some paintings to the king and they entered the royal collection at the time, while others were confiscated from his châteaux during the Revolution and later acquired by the Louvre.

A second important patron in the latter half of the seventeenth century was Cardinal Mazarin, Richelieu's successor as chief minister, whose collection was housed in his apartments in the Louvre and in two galleries, the Galeries Mazarin, now part of the Bibliothèque Nationale. The cardinal's collection, which included Raphael's *Portrait of Castiglione* and *Saint George and Saint Michael*, Titian's *Pardo Venus*, Correggio's *Antiope* and *The Mystical Marriage of St. Catherine*, was further augmented by his purchase of

many works from Charles I of England's collection. On Mazarin's death in 1661, Louis XIV (1638-1715) acquired some of the paintings and sculptures and he purchased others from Mazarin's heirs. Eventually, all these were to be acquired by the Louvre.

The royal collection continued to grow, with diplomatic gifts of paintings from the Venetian Republic, courtiers and princes, and with purchases of Flemish and contemporary French paintings. In 1709 an inventory of the king's collection listed over 2000 items, and a new organization and administration was required to look after them. Placed in charge of the collections was the painter and designer Charles Lebrun who, in addition to being named 'Premier Peintre' was now entitled 'Garde des Tableaux et Dessins du Roi.' The promotion of art had now become the affair of the state and Colbert, minister to Louis XIV, spared no ex-

pense in glorifying the reign of the famous Sun King.

The Louvre now entered a period of intense activity in many directions. In 1648 the Academy of Painting was founded; the first official exhibitions of French art was held in 1667, and from 1673 these exhibitions were held in the Louvre. A drawing school, later the Ecole des Beaux Arts, was also established and in 1681 many of Louis' paintings were placed on semi-public view in the Louvre. Furthermore, during Louis' reign extensive building work on the Louvre itself recommenced. Between 1659 and 1665 Louis le Vau built the north and south wings of the Cour Carrée and in 1661, replacing the Galerie du Roi which had been destroyed by fire in the same year, he built the Galerie d'Apollon.

It seemed that at last the Louvre was nearing completion, but it was still without an exterior façade on the east side. Colbert wished for a triumphal entrance and to this end he announced that the commission was to be awarded to Bernini, the architect of Baroque Rome. Bernini arrived in Paris in 1665, laid the cornerstone of the façade and, like Poussin before him, fled back to Rome. In the end the part known as the 'Colonnade' was entrusted to Claude Perrault, le Vau and Lebrun. Building began in 1667 and was completed by 1670, although the work of decorating the façade continued for the next eight years. Then it abruptly stopped; Louis had decided to move to his

Above Gianlorenzo Bernini: *Bust of Richelieu.* Bernini arrived in Paris in 1665 with a project for an innovatory curved facade to serve as a triumphal entrance, but the colonnade as built was more traditional.

Right Correggio: *Venus, Satyr and Cupid.* The Louvre's collection of High Renaissance works was begun by Francis 1 and greatly expanded by his successors.

palace at Versailles, and from 1678 to 1789 Versailles was to be the principal residence of king and court.

Once again the Louvre began to fall into disrepair. The entrances were turned into shops and stalls, the unfinished parts of the building taken over by squatters, and courtiers moved into the royal apartments, where they altered the interiors to suit their own tastes. Panelling was removed, ceilings altered and skylights let into the attic roof. Structurally and in reputation the Louvre decayed and the area became a center for prostitution and other vice. In an effort to save the building, the city of Paris proposed turning the Louvre into the city hall, but their proposal was rejected by the king.

While Louis XIV lived a very public life, with access to the royal apartments quite easily obtained, court life under his successor Louis XV (1710-74), was more intimate and often it was impossible to view the royal collections, which were now housed in small ill-lit

rooms at Versailles. It was common practice for courtiers to 'borrow' paintings and exhibit them in their own private houses, a custom deplored by many and which led to demands for the building of a special gallery. The Grande Galerie of the Louvre was in no condition to receive works of art, since it was in a dilapidated state and from 1754 its entire space was crowded with a strange collection of plans of fortifications in France. Public opinion was forceful enough to ensure that, in 1775 Jacques Bailly, Keeper of Paintings at Versailles, created a provisional museum in the Queen of Spain's apartments in the Palais du Luxembourg. Opened on October 14th, the collection of 110 paintings could be viewed on Wednesdays and Saturdays, but this was a temporary measure and the exhibition closed in 1779. In the meantime the Comte d'Angevillier, appointed Directeur des Bâtiments du Roi in 1774, was working toward the formation of a museum in the Grande Galerie of the Louvre. He also made regular acquisitions to fill in the gaps in the royal collection, with the aim of making the public more aware of the different schools of painting.

In 1784 the landscape painter Hubert Robert was made Conservateur des Collections du Roi and was given responsibility for fitting out the gallery. No longer used as a royal residence, the Louvre was now invaded by offices, archives and various 'académies.' One such was the Académie Royale de Peinture et Sculpture, which had held its first exhibition in the Louvre in 1725. This took place in the Salon Carré from which comes the term 'salon.'

The principal changes in the building were the alterations to the sloping attic roofs of the Cour Carrée, which were replaced by a flat-roofed story by Ange-Jacques Gabriel in 1754, and the demolition between 1755–74 of any buildings which prevented a clear view of the colonnade. The removal of the old residential area around the Cour Carrée gave Parisians a clear view of the entire façade of the Louvre.

Among the various schemes undertaken to complete the proposed museum was a new monumental staircase in the Grande Galerie leading up to the Salon Carré, which was designed by the architect Jacques-Germain Soufflot and begun in 1781. Decorating and lighting the Grande Galerie (which was finally cleared of all the fortress plans in 1777) took several years. Overhead lighting, already in use in a number of salerooms and private galleries in Paris, was judged to be the most suitable and, as an experiment, the Salon Carré was toplit in 1789. During this period parquet flooring was laid in the Galerie and fire-resisting walls were inserted into the framework of the building. A new and sensational innovation was also added to the Louvre in the form of a lightning conductor. Finally,

Right Hubert Robert's painting of his plans for the Grande Galerie of the Louvre shows it functioning as a museum and art gallery. A landscape painter noted for his picturesque views of ruins, he became keeper of the royal collection in 1784.

to accompany the masterpieces of the collection and as part of the decorative scheme, sculptors were commissioned to make busts of great Frenchmen.

All Paris waited eagerly for the formal re-opening of the Louvre but fate was to forestall this until 1793, for in 1789 France was plunged into the Revolution. In the meantime the art treasures of the crown, the property of the Church and the confiscated possessions of emigrés were kept safe in depositories. In Paris paintings and sculptures from national monuments, especially the churches, were sent to the Convent of the Petits Augustins (now the Ecole des Beaux Arts); confiscated property was held at the Hôtel de Nesles; and the royal collection was sent to the Louvre. From all these treasures, a new museum commission was to select what it felt was likely to be of interest for the museum-to-be. On July 27th, 1793 the Musée Centrale des Arts was created by decree and on August 10th in the same year the Grande Galerie of the Louvre was officially opened, only to be immediately closed for repairs. It was not until April 1799 that the public was admitted, and even then visitors were only allowed into a section of the gallery. The rest of it, following repairs by the architect Reymond, was not opened until July 14th, 1801.

From the outset the guiding concept behind the museum was didactic, reflecting the democratic ideals of the early days of the Revolution, when art was no longer intended solely for the delectation of the privileged classes. For the next 20 years the expanding collections of the Louvre were to reflect the fortune of Napoleon Bonaparte's army, as looted art works arrived from the Low Countries, Germany, Spain and

Above This engraving, dated 1828, shows the east facade, the Colonnade, designed by Perrault, Le Vau and Lebrun.

Right The Grande Galerie in its role as picture gallery in the early nineteenth century, when the Louvre was known as the Musée Napoléon.

Italy. In 1797 a banquet was held in the Grande Galerie in honor of Bonaparte; with the proclamation of the Empire in 1804, the Louvre became known as the 'Musée Napoléon.' Though he added little to the structure of the Louvre, Napoleon did finish the Cour Carrée and provided part of the Grande Galerie with overhead lighting.

By now one of the glories of the Napoleonic Empire, the Louvre attracted visitors from all over the world. But then came the Battle of Waterloo and the end of the Empire in 1815, and a large part of Napoleon's collection, acquired by conquest or treaty, was returned. Fortunately the French had collected well and were able to restock the museum with works sent to the provincial museums for safekeeping.

The new king Louis XVIII (1755-1824) went further to protect the works in the Louvre by decreeing that all those seized during the Revolution were to remain museum property as long as they were kept on view. The completion of the Louvre as a 'palace of the people' was begun under the short-lived Second Republic of 1848 and finally achieved under Napoleon III (1808-73). Restoration and redecoration was overseen by Duban; the Salon Carré and the Salle des Sept Cheminées were given ornamented ceilings; and Eugène Delacroix was commissioned to execute the ceiling painting *Apollo Overcoming the Python* for the vault of the Galerie d'Apollon. At the same time the Département du Peinture was totally reorganized so that paintings were arranged chronologically and works by the same artist were displayed together.

Under Napoleon III the Louvre once again enjoyed a period of magnificence: the old residential area between the Château des Tuileries and the Louvre was demolished on the orders of Baron Haussmann, who transformed a still somewhat medieval Paris into the familiar modern city of wide *boulevards* and *places*. A new building program was initiated by the architect Louis Visconti to join the Louvre with the Tuileries on the north, providing a wing to run parallel to the Grande Galerie and thereby closing the square. At the center of this was the early eighteenth-century Arc du Carousel. Further new wings were built on either side of the Cour Napoléon, providing new large courtyards; the west façade of the Cour Carrée was altered; and, finally, the Grande Galerie was completely lit with overhead lighting. This great phase of building work was completed on August 14th, 1857. Unfortunately Napoleon III was not pleased with the results: for his taste the Louvre was by no means rich enough, and in his view did not properly reflect the prosperity of the Empire or the magnificence of his reign. Therefore in 1861 he ordered Hector Lefuel to cover the palace with sculptures, rebuild the Pavillon de Flore

Above The Louvre in the 1950s viewed from the east, with the Tuileries Gardens behind. The administration of the museum had passed out of the hands of the monarchy during the Commune of 1871.

Left Trucks enter through one of the many gateways giving access to the Louvre, in order to remove the collections for safekeeping during the Second World War.

Right I M Pei's glass pyramid, constructed in the courtyard in 1987–88, with Lemercier's Pavillon de l'Horloge behind. The pyramid was part of a major refurbishment and reorganization of the museum and its collections undertaken by the French government with the support of President Mitterand.

and, strangely, to remove all traces of the old part of the building in the west by demolishing that side of the Grande Galerie, effectively reducing it in size by half.

Having survived without too much damage during the revolutions of 1830 and 1848, the Louvre was not to be so fortunate during the Commune. In 1871 fanatical communards set fire to the Château de Tuileries and the library of the Louvre. Fortunately the fire was brought under control before it could reach the Grande Galerie. In 1883 the charred shell of the Tuileries was demolished, revealing an unbroken view from the Arc du Carousel, the monumental gateway designed by Percier and Fontaine, to the Arc de Triomphe on the Champs Elysées.

During the Commune the administration of the museum passed out of the hands of the sovereign, and was undertaken by a group of artists which included Gustave Courbet, Honoré Daumier and Félix Braquemond. In 1895 the Réunion des Musées nationaux was created, with autonomous financial powers in respect of purchasing works of art for the collection. The Réunion was governed by an assembly, the Conseil des Musées nationaux, which in 1941 was divided into two bodies: an administrative council which was concerned with finance, and an artistic council whose task

was to examine proposals for acquisitions made by the various departmental heads. With a government budget, supplemented by income from entrance fees and legacies (often in lieu of taxes), the Louvre was not only able to continue its policy of acquisition, but also to complete the decorations of the Grande Galerie according to the original scheme by Hubert Robert in 1784.

During the Second World War, the Louvre collection was again evacuated for safe keeping and in 1945, following the end of hostilities, the exhibition rooms were gradually re-opened. The post-war period has witnessed the continued growth of the collection and of the number of galleries: in 1953 Georges Braque's triptych *The Birds* was installed on the ceiling of the Salle Henri II; in 1961 galleries for nineteenth century art were opened on the second floor of the Cour Carrée; and between 1969 and 1971 the Pavillon de Flore and the Aile de Flore were opened. And still the Louvre continues to grow. The latest addition, and no doubt not the last, is a controversial pyramid designed by architect I M Pei and erected in the courtyard of the Louvre, which serves as top-lighting for a new and massive underground entrance and a network of corridors giving access to all parts of the collection.

CHAPTER ONE

The Ancient World

Of the six departments of the Louvre Museum, the first to become autonomous was the Department of Greek and Roman Antiquities, which was created in 1800. Among its many treasures, this department boasts a group of Greek vases from the collection of the Marquis Campana, acquired in 1864 in Rome by the Louvre; the Boscoreale treasure given to the museum by Baron Rothschild in 1898, which comprises more than one hundred pieces of Roman jewelry; and other famous works such as the *Venus de Milo* and the *Nike of Samothrace*, both of which were discovered during archeological excavations in the nineteenth century.

The Department of Egyptian Antiquities was established in 1826 as part of the reorganization of Napoleon Bonaparte's collections. In the same year, Oriental Antiquities was established as a separate section within the museum. It became a department in 1881, rich in the Mesopotamian art brought to the museum from the excavations at Lagash and Mari in the Tigris/Euphrates valley.

The interest in classical art and archeology that provided the impetus for forming these collections has its roots in the culture of the eighteenth century. The seventeenth century had been a period of great scientific and philosophical innovation, and by the eighteenth the impact of science, the growth of religious scepticism and an increased awareness of classical antiquity had all combined to redefine the function of philosophy. Science and secularism inspired the French intellectuals known as the *Philosophes*, who believed that human behavior and institutions could be studied rationally and the faults in them corrected. Asserting the primacy of reason meant turning away from faith and religion and breaking with the Christian world view, which placed doctrine at the center of intellectual activity. Instead of the idea that man should submit himself to what he could know least – the divine – the *Philosophes* invoked the paganism of ancient Greece

Left Venus de Milo, second half of the second century BC copy of a fourth century BC original, one of the most famous of all Greek sculptures.

Right Bronze Etruscan statuette of a *Javelin Thrower*, c.480 BC. The Etruscan culture predated the Roman in Italy.

and Rome, where they believed the spirit of rational inquiry prevailed, at least among educated men.

Artistically, the example of Rome had been important from the 1740s onward. In 1748 Le Normand de Tournheim organized a two-year study tour of Rome for the Marquis de Marigny, his successor as Directeur des Bâtiments at the Louvre. The tour was specifically to train de Marigny in the good and elevated taste that the post was deemed to require, and so he went to Rome to absorb at first hand the new classicizing and antiquarian spirit that was to gather force in the following decades.

Alongside the international movement of Classicism, the international scientific pursuit of archeology began. All of Europe showed an interest in the *scavi* (excavations) that began to be undertaken and the collecting of antiques became a passion, with vast sums of money being spent and new collections formed. For the wealthy and influential intellectual elite of Europe there was a sense of belonging to an international European civilization, albeit a civilization dominated by France and French culture. One of the manifestations of this 'common identity' was the Grand Tour, a period of extended travel on the continent. The highlights naturally included visits to the cities of London, Paris, and Vienna but the monuments of antiquity in Italy were also essential. Not only was the Grand Tour a mark of good breeding, it was looked upon as essential in the 'training' of a man of the world.

Numerous works relating to the rediscovery and re-interpretation of ancient art appeared in the 1750s. Systematic archeological work began with Johann Joachim Winckelmann; his *Gedänken über die Nachahmung der Greichischen Werke*, published in 1755, put forward the view that Greek sculpture was the most worthy standard of aesthetic beauty. Other influential works included the Comte de Caylus's *Recueil des Antiquités* in 1752, Piranesi's *Antichità Romane* in 1756 and, stimulated by the *scavi* in the town of Herculaneum near Naples, the Academia Ercolanese's *Le Pittura Antiche d'Ercolan e Contorni* in 1757. Possibly a more familiar result of this fascination with the antique was Edward Gibbon's monumental study *The Decline and Fall of the Roman Empire*, published between 1776 and 1788.

By far the greatest contributor to the collection of antiquities in the Louvre was Napoleon Bonaparte, whose armies in the last decade of the eighteenth century were advancing through Europe and, especially, Italy. Under the terms of amnesties and treaties, or in lieu of war taxes, works of art were requisitioned by commissions of specialists who made selections of the masterpieces to be sent back to Paris. Armistices agreed with the Dukes of Piacenza and Modena (May 9th and 27th, 1796), a truce signed with the Pope at Bologna (June 8th, 1796) and the Treaty of Tolentino (February 19th, 1797) resulted in the delivery of art treasures from galleries in Parma, Modena, Milan, Cremona, Bologna, Perugia and Rome. Further requisitions from Venice and Rome followed in 1798 and from Florence and Turin in 1800.

On Thermidor 9th and 10th in the Year VI (July, 26-27th, 1798) the arrival of the first consignment of treasures was celebrated in Paris. Brought along the Seine by barge, the captured treasures were unloaded on to wagons near the Jardin des Plantes, taken across Paris and paraded around the Statue of Liberty in the Champs de Mars. Antique Roman sculptures could be seen alongside medals, manuscripts and paintings, all jostling for attention with a menagerie of bears and camels! The 'Antiques' were preceded by a standard which bore the verse:

> La Grèce les céda, Rome les a perdu,
> Leur sort changera deux fois, il ne changera plus.

(Greece gave them up, Rome lost them; twice their fortune has changed, but it will change no more).

In the Louvre the antiques were housed in the apartment formerly belonging to Anne of Austria (under the Galerie d'Apollon) and this section of the museum was opened on Brumaire 18th in the Year IX (November 9th, 1800). In 1812 the Salle des Cariatides, containing the Borghese collection, was opened; its red and white marble decoration was based on Simonetti's design for the Vatican Belvedere for Pope Clement XIV, and was intended to create an atmosphere reminiscent of ancient Rome in the Louvre.

Napoleon was not alone in his search for classical antiquities. During the years 1799-1812 Lord Elgin, the British ambassador to Turkey, obtained permission from the Turkish authorities (who at that time were in control of Greece) to remove substantial portions of the frieze and some of the south metopes from the Parthenon in Athens. These pieces, forming the major part of the 'Elgin Marbles' were transported to Britain and later sold to the British government; they are now in the British Museum. The Louvre has its own section of the Parthenon frieze, however, from the eastern end, which depicts maidens offering the gift of robes for Athena to two officials. Archeology had now emerged from its earlier 'dilettante' status into a professional discipline, but one divided into separate factions with contrary aims. One was concerned with tracing the legends of Judaism and Christianity to their biblical sources, the other with rediscovering the former glories of polytheist Greece and Rome.

By the beginning of the nineteenth century, the treasures of Greece and Rome were competing for museum space with art works from Egypt and other lands. Napoleon's conquest of Egypt in 1798 marked the beginning of a process of discovery and investigation by an unlikely alliance of military authorities and scholars (some would also add art thieves), who uncovered evidence of civilizations even more ancient than those of Greece. The few curious travellers who had visited Egypt in earlier centuries – even those who had left written descriptions and drawings of a land

Right Woman Carrying an Offering, Egyptian, 11th/12th dynasty, c.2000 BC illustrates the stylized elegance of Egyptian art, which combines a degree of realism with the geometric frontality of the original block of stone.

rich in antiquities – had failed to arouse any particular interest in the general public. The Napoleonic occupation of Egypt, although it lasted only three years, brought a dramatic change in Europe's attitude to the country. Both France and its main political rival, Britain, had recognized the strategic importance of Egypt in terms of trade and in the promise of a short trade route to India. But while Britain's interests at the beginning of the nineteenth century remained purely commercial, the French consuls and *savants* who arrived with Napoleon were primarily concerned with Egypt's cultural resources. Having formed themselves into an elite body known as the Institut d'Egypte, they set about researching and publishing the history of the country. The work of the French gave rise to a specialized field within the broad framework of archeology, known as Egyptology. Napoleon, it appears, was its unsuspecting father and while his *savants* accumulated artifacts to send back to the Louvre, the General busied himself with the calculation that the amount of stone in the Great Pyramids at Giza was sufficient to build a defensive wall ten feet high and one foot thick around the whole of France.

Whetting the world's appetite for all things Egyptian was Vivant Denon's book *Voyages dans la basse et la haute Egypte*, published in 1804. Denon accompanied General Descaix on his river journey to Aswan, when the islands of Philae and Elephantine were discovered, and took advantage of his official duties as illustrator to the Institute by bringing out his own book. Further excitement was caused by Jean-François Champollion, who supplied the key to deciphering Egyptian hieroglyphic script in 1822. The Rosetta Stone, now in the British Museum, was found in 1799 by one of Napoleon's officers, Lieutenant Bouchard. The French were smart enough to take a wax impression before losing possession of the stone. It was inscribed with 14 lines of hieroglyphics, 32 lines of 'demotic' or everyday Greek script and 54 lines of 'hieratic' Greek script. It became evident to Champollion that the same thing was being written in three different ways: a record of the honors bestowed on Pharoah Ptolemy Epiphanes.

European interest in Egypt was such that there now started an almost international race to excavate. King Frederick William of Prussia financed an expedition between 1843 and 1845 to survey the Nile from the Delta to Khartoum and on into Ethiopia. In the process thousands of items were removed from their historical setting and placed in magnificent Egyptian galleries in the Prussian Imperial Museum. Further French-sponsored excavations were carried out at the Serapeum (temple to Serapis) at Saqqara, at Memphis and Abydos by Auguste Edouard Mariette. In 1882 Britain invaded Egypt and became the *de facto* ruler of the country. With this, the task of uncovering Egypt's past effectively passed into the hands of British archeologists like Flinders Petrie and, later, George Herbert (the Earl of Caernarvon) and Edward Carter, discoverers of Tutankhamun's tomb.

The first practical steps in the rediscovery of lost Mesopotamian civilizations – places and peoples mentioned in classical literature and biblical legend such as Nimrud, Nineveh and Babylon – were carried out by an Italian nobleman, Pietro della Valle. In 1621, ostensibly to mend his broken heart, della Valle visited Persepolis in Persia, identified four years earlier as the city of Darius, where he copied an inscription carved on a rockface in the wedge-shaped characters of 'cuneiform,' a written language whose system and meaning were unknown. Inscribed clay bricks and tablets and other curiosities which Valle sent back home to Rome were eventually to allow scholars to decipher this most ancient of written languages.

Other travellers followed in della Valle's footsteps: Jean Chardin and Jean Baptiste Tavernier, who were traders in precious gemstones, and the Abbé de Beauchamp, the Pope's Vicar-General in Baghdad, all hired workmen to dig at Babylon. While this was a resourceful beginning, more work was needed before even the youngest nations of Mesopotamian antiquity could be identified and located with certainty. In the 1850s *Travels and Researches in Chaldea and Susiana* by Kennett Loftus, published after the author's investigations at Warka (biblical Erech or Uruk), Sankara (the Ellasor of the *Book of Genesis*) and Tell el-Muqaiyar (Ur of the Chaldeas, the reputed birthplace of Abraham), caused a new wave of enthusiasm in France, Britain and America for properly financed and organized excavations in Mesopotamia.

In 1877, the French Vice-Consul at Basra, Ernest de Sarzec, applied to the Wali of Basra for permission to dig at Tell Tollah, at that time believed to be the site of the Sumerian city of Lagash (recent excavations have shown it to be the site of the adjacent city of Girsu). In two seasons of digging, de Sarzec produced a vast haul of magnificent diorite statues and thousands of inscribed cylinders and tablets, representing the largest ever imperial library in the ancient world. All these de Sarzec sold to the Louvre for 130,000 francs.

During the next nine seasons of excavations at Tell Tollah, one of the richest of all Mesopotamian sites, several thousands of artifacts found their way into the hands of dealers in Baghdad and Basra, the centers of illegal trade in antiquities. It is more than likely that many items remain unknown and unrecorded in private ownership. From Mesopotamian excavations, archeologists found that, even at the very earliest stages of a community's existence, sculptors, jewelers and metalsmiths were using sophisticated skills and techniques such as sand casting and lost wax casting.

In 1836 Sir Austen Leyard, who was born in Paris of Huguenot parents, set off on his travels with the intention of going to Ceylon. The temptation to stay in the Near East, however, proved overwhelming.

Left This sixth-century BC bronze warrior from northern Italy shows none of the growing Greek interest in naturalism in its representation of the human body.

Above This Sassanian Persian horse's head in silver and gold from the fourth/fifth century AD was part of the decoration on the royal throne, and is characteristic of the Sassanian predilection for animal forms.

Leyard went to Kermanshah in Persia, where he met two French artists, Flandin and Coste, who had been sent from Paris to the Tehran legation and were busy drawing the sculptures of the region. Thrown together in a brief period of Anglo-French cordiality, Leyard and his companions seemed somewhat indifferent to the monumental pictorial art that surrounded them – the monumental sculptures of Taki-Bostram portraying Sassanian kings and hunting themes. Cordiality was soon to turn into rivalry however, encouraged by the demands of national museums and the political ambitions of European empires, and competitive and often destructive excavations were undertaken.

The search for the city of Nineveh had already been started at Kuyunjik by the French Consul at Mosul, Paul Emile Botta. But Botta believed he had discovered a more rewarding site to the north, at Khorsabad, and proposed to continue his research there. While Leyard was unsuccessfully petitioning the British government and the British Museum for funds,

the French government undertook to finance Botta's excavations as soon as he began to make sensational finds. Huge stone figures and sculpted slabs from Khorsabad, the first of the great monuments of the northern palace of Sargon II, king of Assyria (c.710 BC), some weighing in excess of twenty tons, were hauled by up to six hundred men on carts to Mosul. From there they were floated on rafts along the one thousand miles of the Tigris to Basra and thence by ship to France, where excited crowds awaited their arrival at the Louvre.

In 1854 France renewed her interest in Persia and the ruins of Susa were investigated by Marcel Dieulafoy and his wife. In 1877 France was given permission by the Shah of Persia to excavate 'in perpetuity'. In 1901 at Susa, the French found perhaps the most important document of the ancient world, the *Law Code of Hammurabi*. This diorite stele was topped by a bas-relief depicting King Hammurabi of Babylon receiving the commission to write the laws from the sun-god Shamash, who was also the god of justice. Written on both sides of the stele, the code was the basis for the law in Babylonia, Assyria and many other surrounding states and ultimately for Talmudic law and many of the statutes of the Christian world. In fact many of the laws from the *Code of Hammurabi* have passed unchanged into the everyday codes of conduct in use today in many parts of the world. Murder was the subject of the first laws; false accusations were regarded as seriously as the actual crime itself; theft, marital rights and the obligation of wives, husbands, children and parents were all explained in terms of right and wrong.

All that was missing now for many Europeans was material evidence to support Old Testament accounts of the Israelites, and even this was finally supplied by Flinders Petrie's discovery of a temple inscription from Thebes in Egypt. A hymn of praise to Pharoah Merenptah (ruled from 1234 BC), the inscription cites a number of victories over Libyan tribes and, for the first time in historical records, mention is made of Israel, proving conclusively that the Israelites were in the land of Canaan in the thirteenth century BC.

This discovery proved to be of enormous interest to the scientific investigators in Palestine. In 1860 Napoleon III commissioned Renan to investigate ancient Phoenicia (modern Lebanon), and he excavated at Tyre and Sidon. Renan's contribution to this mission was largely limited to his book *La Vie de Jésus* and it was Félicien de Saulcy who began excavations proper in Palestine. Having gone to Jerusalem in 1850 to seek solace following his wife's death, de Saulcy set out to find Sodom and Gomorrah. In Jerusalem he investigated the rock-cut burial chambers to the north of the city, known popularly as the Tombs of the Kings, and jumped to the conclusion that a fragment of sarcophagus lid was the cover to King David's coffin. Several other sarcophagi were sent to the Louvre, one of them inscribed with the name of Queen Sadan or Sadah, whose identity remains a mystery.

A second Frenchman in Palestine was Charles Clermont-Ganneau, whose most important contribution both to ancient history and the Louvre collection of antiquities was his recovery in 1868 of the famous Moabite Stone or the *Mesha Stele*, as it is usually called. This stele, which had been smashed by tribesmen who had been refused the usual reward following their find, was reconstructed by Ganneau. The inscription of the stele commemorates victories by Mesha, king of the Moabs, over Israel in the ninth century BC, when the land was divided into the northern kingdom, Israel, with its capital at Samaria, and the southern kingdom of Judea based on Jerusalem.

The stele had originally been found by an Alsatian missionary, Frederick Augustus Klein, and ownership was disputed. The French claimed it, since Klein was born a Frenchman; the British, for reasons known only to themselves, claimed it as well; while the Prussians sent a Professor Lepsius to buy the stone from Klein. In the meantime the actual finders of the stone and therefore the tribal owners, the Bani-Hamadiyya, who still had not been paid for their work, decided that the cause of the delay was an evil *jinn* which lived inside the stone. To rid the stele of the bad luck, the Bani-Hamadiyya alternately heated the stone over a fire and immersed it in cold water until it split open. The *jinn* was released but the stele was shattered.

Ganneau appears to have been farsighted enough to have made a 'squeeze' (a paper impression) of the inscription and, having combed the ground for fragments, he reassembled the stele, replacing missing parts with plaster casts obtained from the 'squeeze'. In 1873 the reconstructed diorite and plaster stele of Mesha went on show at the Louvre, where academic debate regarding its inscription, its importance and even its authenticity continued to rage.

By the end of the nineteenth century, French archeology had been officially represented in Egypt and Palestine for nearly 100 years and had supported excavations in Greece since the early 1800s. During the twentieth century research by the French continued at Mari on the river Euphrates. Begun in 1933, these excavations revealed one of the principal settlements of Mesopotamia from the period of Hammurabi of Babylon, and the finds are now on display in the Egyptian department of the Louvre Museum.

Left
Stele of King Zet, c.3000 BC
Limestone bas relief, 95¾ inches high
(245 cm)

King Zet is known as the 'Serpent
King' after the serpent that served as
the hieroglyph for his name. This
stele, found in the king's tomb at
Abydos, was a symbol of royalty.

On the stele is depicted the image of
a falcon in profile. The bird was the
symbol of the god Horus and was the
incarnation of Egyptian kingship.
The falcon is shown standing on top
of two doorways of a palace, a device
which symbolizes an earlier phase of
the Egyptian kingdom when Egypt
was ruled by two Pharoahs, one in
Upper Egypt and one in Lower
Egypt.

Above
Navigation Scene
(Tomb Furniture), Mid Empire
Painted wood, 15 × 31½ inches
(38.5 × 81 cm)

The tombs of the influential in ancient
Egypt were commonly decorated and
furnished with scenes showing the
ritual and religious aspects of death
and the funeral, and the secular activities of the owner during his lifetime.
These objects had a magical as well as
religious function. The Egyptians
believed that the *Ka* or spirit of the
deceased had to be provided for in the
afterlife with food, drink, equipment,
even entertainment and transport.
Even if the deceased's family failed to
undertake the required rituals after
death, the tomb offerings and accom-
panying paintings and inscriptions
would ensure that, in the 'House of
the *Ka*', these rituals were carried out
for eternity.

Above left
The Priest Ebih-Il of the Temple of Ishtar, c.2900-2685 BC (?)
Alabaster with bitumen inlays (eyebrows) and lapis lazuli (eyes). From Mari, now called Tell-Hariri on the River Euphrates. 20½ inches high (52 cm)

This small statue dates from what is known as the Fara period in Sumer, and was found in the temple of the goddess Ishtar, close to that of the king. Characteristic of the work of this period are the large eyes, here laid with lapis lazuli, a semi-precious stone. The workmanship is particularly accomplished and the alabaster used is of an unusually fine grain. The carefully dressed beard, prominent cheekbones and somewhat malicious smile give the statue a very individual character. Like Egyptian statues, this piece has been conceived frontally, although it is less rigid than contemporary Egyptian work.

Above right
Goddess of Fertility, second half of the third millenium BC
Terracotta plaque with red varnish, from Cyprus, 25 inches high (63.5 cm)

During the Bronze Age, the culture on the island of Cyprus was closely related to those on the Anatolian (southern Turkish) coast and in the region of Syria. At the same time, Cyprus' geographical location also allowed for contacts with the civilization and culture of the Aegean. One of the oldest examples of geometric stylization of the human figure, this representation of a goddess is simply a flat clay rectangle in which incisions have been made to indicate arms and mouth, clothing and jewels. Only the ears and the nose project from the surface.

Right
Raherka and Mersankh (family tomb group), Fifth Dynasty 2563-2423 BC
Painted limestone, 20⅘ inches high (52.5 cm)

Much of Egyptian art was produced primarily for religious purposes, in particular to aid the *Ka* or spirit of the deceased in its journey to the afterlife. One type of funeral or mortuary statue characteristic of the Old Kingdom is the family group. Here the figures were conceived as separate entities and then placed together. Sometimes 'false' groups were created, where two statues representing the same person were paired. In the group of Raherka and Mersankh, the pair have a much more naturalistic appearance, with the woman holding the man's arm. Raherka, the chief scribe, is painted in red ocher, his wife Mersankh in yellow.

Left
Seated Scribe, Fifth Dynasty
2563–2423 BC, circa 2500 BC, from
Sakkara
Painted limestone, 21 inches high
(53 cm)

This statue of an unnamed scribe was
discovered in the course of the mid-
nineteenth-century excavations at
Sakkara organized by the French
Egyptologist Auguste Edouard
Mariette. Considered to be one of the
masterpieces of Egyptian art, the
figure is on the one hand realistic –
particularly in the gaze of the eyes,
which are of polished inlaid stones –
while on the other hand it is conceived
geometrically, retaining the required
frontality, and the back, with its flat
planes, preserves the original cube or
stone block from which the figure has
been carved.

In 1921, this figure was found to
bear a very close resemblance to a
seated statue of the monarch Kai,
which had also come from Mariette's
excavations and had also been sent to
the Louvre.

Above
**Stele of the Victory of
Naramsu'en, King of Akkad,**
2389–2353 BC
Pink sandstone, from Susa, 78⅘ × 41⅓
inches (198× 104 cm)

This commemorative stele was taken
from Susa as war plunder in the
twelfth century BC by King Shutruk-
nahhunte, after the Babylonians had
conquered the city of Sippar. The
stele of Naramsu'en is an exceptional
monument in that it is believed to be
the oldest attempt at the representation of space. The scene shows the
Akkadian king of Mesopotamia and
his forces attacking a hill tribe. Leading the expedition is the king himself:
not only is he the largest figure to be
represented, he is also depicted wearing an elaborate crown. Only the
enemy are shown as falling or dying,
while the Akkadian troops remain
triumphantly alive, since this is a
commemorative piece and something
of an early propaganda exercise!

Also inscribed on the stele is a written record of events in cuneiform, the
first written language based on
abstract signs. Each sign represents
both an object and a spoken sound, a
syllable: a major step in the development of alphabetic writing.

Above
Sphinx from Tanis, Middle
Kingdom, c.2134–1785 BC
Red granite, 81 × 136 inches
(208 × 526.5 cm)

Next to the pyramids at Giza, the
sphinx is probably the most enduring
symbol from and of Ancient Egypt.
With the head of a man or woman and
the body of a recumbent lion, front
paws outstretched, the sphinx combines physical and intellectual
strength, the political and spiritual
power incarnate in the Pharoah.

Sphinxes come in variety of guises:
the sphinx from Tanis, with its
human head, is known as an andro-
sphinx; the criosphinx has a ram's
head and denotes silence while the
heirosphinx is falcon-headed and refers to the sun. Here the sphinx wears
the *nemes* head-dress with the accom-
panying *uraeus*, symbolic of power
and sovereignty, as well as a short
false, square beard. On its chest, inscribed in a cartouche, are hiero-
glyphs, the Egyptian hieratic script
used only for religious and royal
records.

Above center
Statue of Chancellor Nakht,
Middle Kingdom, Twelfth
Dynasty (1991–1786 BC)
Painted wood with inlaid eyes,
69 inches high (162 cm)

This statue, found at Assuit, is one of
the most remarkable pieces of
wooden sculpture to be preserved
from the Middle Kingdom. It still retains traces of its original poly-
chromy, as well as the red body color
which almost entirely covers the
figure. The statue follows the tradi-

tions of the Old Kingdom in its frontal stance, the left leg advanced and both arms held rigidly at the side of the body. The figure was designed to be viewed from the front, but the quality of the carving gives it an extraordinary presence whatever angle it is viewed from. In a similarly geometric way, the treatment of the long skirt is rather like a truncated pyramid.

Fully painted to resemble skin, hair and clothing, and with its inlaid eyes, the figure of the Chancellor must have looked incredibly impressive, not to say lifelike.

Above right
Code of Hammurabi, King of Babylon, c.1930–1888 BC
Black basalt, from Susa, 88½ inches high (222.5 cm)

After centuries of turmoil, the Babylonians became masters of all Mesopotamia around 1700 BC. The founder of this Babylonian dynasty and first ruler of Mesopatamia was Hammurabi, who was both a king and a 'god', a divine ruler on earth. Hammurabi's most memorable achievement was his law code, one of the earliest systematic, written bodies of law in the world. The law code was engraved on a tall slab of basalt. At the top of this, in a deeply carved relief against a flat background, Hammurabi is shown before the enthroned sun-god Shamash, who holds a scepter in his right hand and has flames issuing from his shoulders. It appears that Shamash is handing the king the scepter, the symbol of power. Beneath this scene is carved the law code itself, which is quite reasonable and surprisingly humane, and covers every aspect of both public and private life.

Left
Draped Female Torso, end of
Eighteenth Dynasty (1370-60 BC)
Red quartz, probably from Tell el
Amarna, 11⅘ inches high (30.2 cm)

This fragment of a statue of a female
figure is typical of the Amarna style
with its prominent abdomen and
thighs as well as the linear quality of
the drapery. The linear style has its
origins very early in Egyptian art but
by the Eighteenth Dynasty was widespread. The modelling of the stomach
and thighs, with their rounded sur-
faces, is a regular feature of pharaonic
iconography, the source of which is
thought to be the supposed physical
deformity of Ikhnaton.

On this piece, the drapery has been
indicated by incising lines on to the
stone, as compared to the later Ptole-
maic *Torso of Isis*, where the drapery is
modeled.

Above
**Necklace of the Pharoah
Pinedjem**, Twenty-first Dynasty,
c. 1030 BC
Gold, silver and lapis lazuli, Thebes,
19⅗ inches long (50 cm)

This fabulous Theban necklace dates
from the New Kingdom, a period
which also includes the famous treasure of the Pharoah Tutenkhamun.
While most Egyptian art was
governed by strictly formal stylistic
rules, jewelers appear to have taken
great pleasure in richly decorative
ornamental design for its own sake.

Pinedjem's necklace also demon-
strates the high degree of technical skill
that Egyptian craftsmen achieved, apparent in the fine links of the triple
gold chain, the elegant lotus-shaped
pendants, and the rectangular plaque
decorated with the image of the sacred
scarab crowned with a solar disk. To
the Egyptians, the scarab or dung
beetle was a symbol of immortality
and divine wisdom. Furthermore, all
scarabs were thought to be male and
thus represented virility and the gen-
erative power of life.

Left above
Propitiatory Genius of a Hero,
usually identified as Gilgamesh,
end of the eighth century BC
Alabaster, 166½ inches high (419.6 cm)

Around 900 BC all of Mesopotamia
was ruled by the powerful and
efficient state machinery of the Assyr-
ians, whose magnificent royal palaces
grew to an unprecedented size. This
alabaster relief of an individual divin-
ity, hero, prince or 'genius', (some
say the hero Gilgamesh) comes from
the palace of King Sargon II in Dur
Sharruukin (ancient Khorsabad),
where it was originally placed in one
of the inner rooms which contained
the king's throne.

Left below
**The Pharoah Taharka Offering
Two Wine Cups to the Falcon
God Hemen**, Twenty-fifth
Dynasty, c.689–680 BC
Schist, wood, bronze with base covered
in silver, and falcon gilded. 7⅘ inches
high × 4 inches wide × 10¼ inches long
(20 × 10 × 26cm)

While bronze sculpture had flourished
in Mesopotamia, it did not appear in
Egypt until after the Twenty-second
Dynasty, about 1085 BC. In Egypt the
falcon was the King of Birds and the
main species used for hunting and also
represented the god all–seeing Horus.

Right
Head of a Horseman (the Rampin
Head), sixth century BC
Marble with traces of polychrome,
11⅖ inches (28 cm)

It is only recently that this head, found
on the Acropolis, Athens, was recognized as belonging to the fragments of
an equestrian statue in the National
Museum in Athens. The Louvre head
is now mounted on a plaster copy of
the original body and horse. The head
dates from the period of the tyrant
Pisistratus, when Athens was under
the artistic influence of the Ionian
regions. Although belonging to the
Archaic period in Greek art and wearing the characteristic archaic smile,
the head of the horseman twists
slightly to the left, a move away from
the rigid conventions of frontality.

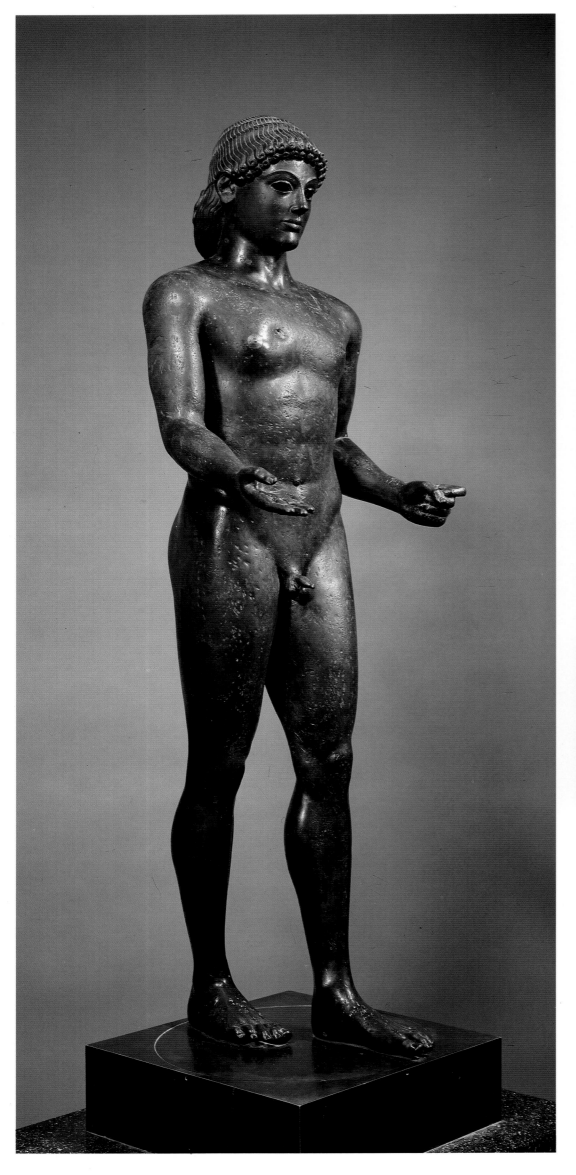

Left
Piombino Apollo, second half of
the fifth century BC
Bronze, 49¼ inches high (128 cm)

This famous bronze figure of a standing youth was retrieved from the sea
at Piombino, Italy in 1832 and is associated with the god Apollo, since the
left hand is outstretched as though it
was holding a bow and arrow. The
eyesockets are now empty, but
originally they would have contained
'false' eyes of colored paste or stone.

The figure's nipples, lips and eyebrows are indicated by red copper, while under the right foot an inscription in silver, written in the Doric dialect, states that the statue was dedicated in Athens as part of a tithe payment.

While this bronze displays a human body represented relatively naturalistically in the developing classical tradition, it is still possible to see the traces of archaic Greek artistic conventions in the figure's frontality, symmetry and the advanced left leg.

Above
Sarcophagus from Cerveteri,
c. 550 BC
Painted terracotta, 78 × 46 inches
(197.5 × 115 cm)

This painted terracotta sarcophagus was found in the necropolis of ancient Caere, a focus of the Etruscan civilization which was the precursor of ancient Rome. The sarcophagus is covered by a lid decorated with the figures of a husband and wife reclining on a Greek couch (*kline*). The

Etruscans saw these as representations of the deceased at an everlasting banquet since, like the Egyptians, they believed that the afterlife was a prolongation of earthly life. The woman's brimmed hat and her shoes with their upturned toes (*calcei repandi*) are typically Etruscan, yet stylistically the work is related to Ionian sculpture. The monumentality of the figures, the slanting, almond-shaped eyes and the archaic smile are features which can also be seen in the *Rampin Head* (page 38).

Archers of the Persian Guard,
fifth century BC
Frieze from the Palace of Darius at Susa, detail. Enameled bricks, height of each archer 57⅘ inches (142.5 cm)

The ancient Mesopotamian tradition of using enameled bricks for surface ornament and architectural reliefs was used by the late Babylonians to distinctive effect, particularly in the Ishtar Gate of King Nebuchadnezzar's sacred precinct in Babylon. (The restored Ishtar Gate is now in the State Museum, Berlin.) The use of baked and glazed bricks was continued by the Persian kings in the decoration of their luxurious palaces.

This frieze of archers, the famous 'Immortals' carrying lances with gold and silver tips, comes from the palace of Darius, the self styled 'King of Kings', at Susa.

Above
Ganymede with a Hoop,
Berlin Painter
Attic red-figure krater, c.480-470 BC
13 inches high, 13 inches in diameter at krater's mouth (33 × 33 cm)

There are over 200 vases ascribed to the nameless Berlin Painter, called after an amphora now in the museum in Berlin. The Berlin Painter belonged to the second generation of red-figure ware painters, at a time when the influence of Ionic art was waning and the increasing naturalism of Attic sculpture was taking over as the main inspiration for vase painting. Here the figure is shown in a three-quarter view, with a wealth of anatomical detail indicated by fine red lines. Some lines are in paler reds which allow for subtle shading. Ganymede was a human boy whose beauty moved Zeus, in the guise of an eagle, to carry him off as his cup-bearer. Here Ganymede is shown rolling a hoop, while in his left hand he holds a cockerel.

Left

Artemis of Gabies, known as *Diana of Versailles*, attributed to Praxiteles, c.350–330 BC
Roman copy in Parian marble, found at Gabies, Tunisia in 1792, 95½ inches high (165 cm)

Praxiteles, alongside Phidias, must rank as the best known sculptor of ancient Greece, even though much of his work is known only through Roman reproductions, such as this figure of Artemis from Tunisia. In 345, on his return from Asia Minor, Praxiteles was charged with making this largescale figure of the goddess for the sanctuary at the Acropolis in Athens.

According to legend Artemis, the daughter of Zeus and Leto (one of the Titans), was the slightly older twin sister of Apollo. She was the eternal virgin and the huntress goddess, whose Roman equivalent was Diana and whose animal familiars were stags and bees. Artemis' temple at Ephesus, where she was worshipped as a 'mother goddess', was renowned as one of the Seven Wonders of the Ancient World.

Right

Nike of Samothrace, c.190 BC
Parian marble, 128 inches high (328 cm)

The winged *Nike* (Victory) was found in Samothrace in 1863 and was for a number of years connected with the naval victory of Demetrius Poliorcetes in 306 and then with the conquest of Rhodes by Antiochus III (222–187 BC). Stylistically, the later victory is more appropriate. The *Nike* is a spectacular piece: portrayed standing on the prow of a ship, the sea wind catching her drapery, she is the embodiment of triumph. The treatment of the drapery, which clings to her body and billows out behind, is related to the so-called 'wet drapery' of the post-Phidian period after the fifth century BC.

The *Nike of Samothrace* dates from the last phase of Greek art, known as 'Hellenistic', from c.330–100 BC, when Greek art moved towards increased realism in modelling and movement, in expression and in the range of subjects treated.

duce accurate copies of Greek statues before these were melted down. The mechanical method of copying by the 'pointing process' (still used today) meant that, from a cast of a statue or relief, many marble copies could be made with considerable accuracy by transferring points from cast to marble block.

Greek artists in the service of Rome produced numerous copies of statues for the adornment of public places and private houses. Without these copies, our knowledge of Greek sculpture would be very meager.

Right
Portrait of a Woman, second century AD
Encaustic on wood, 16½ × 9⅖ inches (42.2 × 24 cm)

There are around 200 of these paintings, the only examples of easel paintings from the ancient world. Painted on wood, often imported cedar or sycamore, these funerary portraits from Fayum in Egypt are believed to represent members of well-to-do 'hellenized' families who settled in Egypt and adopted the local burial traditions, including mummification. They may have been produced during the subjects' life and one controversial theory suggests that these portraits were displayed in the house before being attached to the mummy. The individuality displayed by each portrait suggests that, even if they were not painted during the sitter's lifetime, then the artist was at least acquainted with his subject.

In many ways, these funerary portraits can be seen as the prototypes for Byzantine icons in the full-face representation, the immense and dark eyes and the somewhat melancholy expression. The technique of encaustic painting requires melted colored beeswax to be spread on the surface of the board with a spatula. The artist has to work quickly, using short strokes and dabs to create the forms without outlines. This technique, both more difficult and often less versatile than other painting media, does however produce incredibly luminous effects.

Above
The Borghese Gladiator, first century BC
Marble, 77¾ inches (199 cm)

This statue of a gladiator is signed on the tree trunk which serves as a supporting device: Agasias, son of Dositheus, from Ephesus. It is a Roman copy of a Greek work; the original statue is likely to have been in bronze, a material valuable to the Romans for their weaponry. Fortunately by 100 BC they were able to pro-

CHAPTER TWO

Early Christian to Renaissance

In 323 AD Constantine the Great made the fateful decision to move the capital of the Roman Empire to the Greek town of Byzantium, renamed Constantinople (now Istanbul) in his honor. As well as acknowledging the strategic and economic importance of the eastern provinces, Constantinople, situated at the heart of the most Christian area of the empire, was also symbolic of the Christian basis of the Roman state. Within a century, however, the empire was split: the western provinces fell under sucessive waves of invading Germanic tribes – Visigoths, Vandals, Ostrogoths and Lombards – and by the end of the sixth century had entered a period of relative artistic diversity, the so-called Dark Ages.

In contrast, the Eastern Empire of Byzantium survived the onslaughts and reached a new height of power and stability under Justinian (527-565 AD). One hundred years later, however, with the rise of Islam, the African and near eastern parts of the empire fell to conquering Arabs. By the eleventh century, Turkish forces had occupied a large part of Asia Minor and the last Byzantine possessions in the west, in southern Italy, fell to the Normans. Despite these losses the Byzantine Empire, now reduced to the Balkans and Greece, was maintained until 1453, when Constantinople finally fell to the Turks.

The division of the Roman Empire also led to a religious schism. At the time of Constantine, the Bishop of Rome was the acknowledged head or Pope of the Christian church, deriving his authority from St Peter. This claim was disputed in the East, however, and the differences in doctrine which developed led to the division of Christendom into the western or Catholic Church and the eastern Orthodox Church. While Roman Catholicism maintained its independence from imperial or state authority, the Orthodox Church in contrast was based on a union of spiritual and secular power personified by the emperor.

The splitting of the empire into two makes it impossible to discuss the art of the period under a single blanket heading. The term 'Early Christian' does not really define a style but refers rather to works of art produced for, or by, Christians in the first five centuries AD, prior to the schism. On the other hand, the term 'Byzantine' designates not only the art of the eastern empire but also a specific style.

The study of Byzantine art was begun as early as the seventeenth century by two French scholars, L'Abbé and du Carge, but the prestige of Rome for a long time blocked the way to accurate assessment and true appreciation. Byzantine art can be divided into three main periods. The First Golden Age lasted from the reign of Justinian in 527 to the outbreak of the Iconoclast Crisis in the eighth century, when an edict of 726 AD prohibiting religious imagery caused the systematic destruction of works of art that are now known to us only from descriptions. The period of the Macedonian and Commene emperors, from the ninth to the twelfth century, and the Palaeologue renaissance from the thirteenth to the fifteenth century together correspond to what is generally called the Second Golden Age.

The Emperor Justinian himself was a patron of the arts unmatched since Constantine's day, and among the surviving buildings of his reign by far the greatest is Hagia Sophia (the Church of the Holy Wisdom) in Istanbul, built between 532 and 537. While the buildings of the sixth century show no attempt at exterior decoration, inside the basilicas painting flourished in all its forms – mosaics (which at Hagia Sophia were whitewashed over by the Moslem Turks in 1453 and only uncovered in 1932), frescoes, and icons (though again, because of their fragility and the numerous earth tremors in the region, many have disappeared).

The majority of extant works from the First Golden Age consists of manuscripts, goldsmiths' work, textiles (Justinian started a silk industry at Byzantium in 522), and above all ivory carvings. Many different objects were decorated with great skill: furniture, caskets and pyxes, missal covers, diptyches – like the Louvre's *Barberini Ivory* – and portable icons like the *Harbaville Triptych*.

The further development of Byzantine art after the age of Justinian was halted by the Iconoclast Controversy, which began with an imperial edict prohibiting the production of religious artworks, issued in 726 by Leo III the Isaurian (717-740), and was furthered by his son Constantine V Copronymous (740-775). The roots of the controversy were deep and in the main had a political background, reflecting a power struggle between state and church. Leo III was concerned not so much with the purity of religion – even though it seemed to many that the veneration of religious images

Above The *Baptistery of Saint Louis* was made in Syria or Egypt and signed Mohammed Ibn el-Zain. It is made of chiseled and repoussé copper inlaid with silver.

had developed into something close to idolatry – as with the increasing power, both political and financial, of the monasteries. The problem Leo saw was in the intimate relationship between the monks and the common people. The monasteries, as well as being places of worship and pilgrimage, also housed relics of miracle-working saints from which they derived an income in the form of selling 'cures,' charms and saintly souvenirs. Furthermore, the monasteries were also the largest landowners and enjoyed a tax-free existence. As a result of the rather comfortable life they offered, and particularly since the inmates were exempt from military service, the religious houses succeeded in luring young men away from active service in Leo's under-strength army, thus thwarting his hopes for a strong military state. Additionally, endowments and donations to the monasteries were depriving the state of considerable revenue. Leo, by forbidding the worship of images, deprived the monasteries of one of their most effective sources of income and propaganda, a measure that affected them not only as owners and custodians of religious artworks, but also as manufacturers.

While the edict successfully reduced the number of religious images produced, it failed to abolish production completely. The purely decorative tasks to which

artists were restricted during the hundred years or so of the controversy brought a return to a more naturalistic 'hellenistic' style and made for a more vigorous treatment of subjects such as hunting or garden scenes, in which the human figure is depicted less rigidly, and in a less flat and 'frontal' style, than previously. Following the victory of the 'iconophiles' in 843, when the Empress Theodora restored orthodoxy, the Second Golden Age of Byzantine art in the ninth and tenth centuries continued these naturalistic achievements and applied them to ecclesiastical art. Later Byzantine art once again became formally stereotyped under the influence of monastic orthodoxy. The resulting conservativism was such that icons of the Greek Orthodox monasteries were still, in the seventeenth century, being painted in the same manner as they had been in the eleventh.

The reconquest of the lost western provinces of the empire remained a serious political goal for the Byzantine emperors until the middle of the seventh century, but the possibility ceased to exist when they were faced with a new threat from the east in the form of the Arabs, under the banner of Islam. By 732 the Arabs, having overrun the Byzantine Near-Eastern and African provinces, had occupied North Africa and most of Spain and were threatening south-western France.

Left exposed and unprotected, western Europe was forced to develop its own political framework. The Roman Church, having severed ties with the east, turned for support to the Germanic north, where a

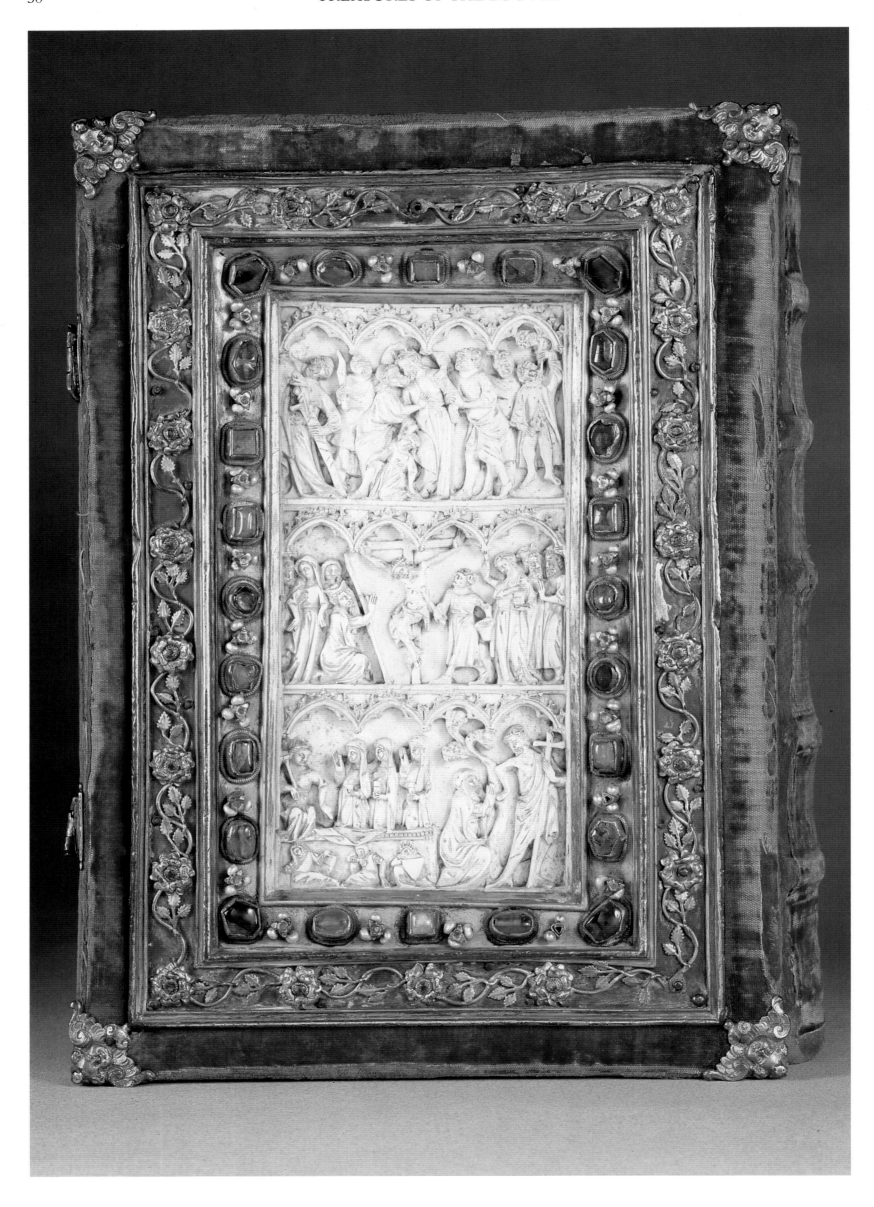

Frankish kingdom was ruled by the Carolingian dynasty. Charles Martel (714-741) saved Gaul from Arab invasion at Poitiers in 732 and won over the Germans to Christianity, while Pepin the Short (741-768) completed the conquest of Gaul and defended the Pope against the Lombards by presenting him in 756 with the territory that was to form the basis of the papal states. These reigns laid the foundations of Carolingian power and prepared the way for the first Holy Roman Emperor, Charlemagne (768-814). Crowned in Rome by the Pope in 800, Charlemagne created a European civilization which stretched from Holstein to Barcelona and Benevento and from the Elbe to the Atlantic, with its capital at the center in Aachen, where the borders of Belgium, the Netherlands and Germany meet today. Whereas in Byzantium the emperor in Constantinople had always ratified newly elected popes, in the west the legitimacy of the Catholic emperor depended on the Church.

Of all the artworks of the Carolingian renaissance the finest achievements were undoubtedly in manuscript illuminations, the favorite themes for which included initials and ornamental borders, Evangelical figures and royal portraits, with the bodies depicted in a more three-dimensional reality than Byzantine works. Along with the imperial title Charlemagne also attempted to restore ancient Roman civilization, of which the preservation of the 'classics' of literature was an important part. The oldest surviving texts of many of the classical Latin authors are to be found in Carolingian manuscripts, which until recently were mistakenly regarded as Roman. The minor arts also indicate a revival of Roman style; the bronze equestrian statuette of Charlemagne in the Louvre shows the Christian king mounted on his horse in the manner of Roman emperors.

Charlemagne's descendants, Louis the Pious (814-840), Charles the Bald (840-877), Louis the Stammerer, Louis III and Charles the Fat (880-887), were unable to preserve the unity of the Empire. By 888, the ambitions of the Church to control the civil power, coupled with Norman, Hungarian and Arab invasions, led to the break-up of the Empire. From its ruins rose the nations of France, Germany and Italy.

During the eleventh century the Normans assumed a major role in shaping the political and cultural destiny of Europe. William the Conqueror was proclaimed king of England in 1066, while other Norman nobles busied themselves with clearing out the Arabs from Sicily and the Byzantines from southern Italy. In Germany, after the death of the last Carolingian monarch in 911, the center of political power shifted north to Saxony, with the Ottonian dynasty founded in 919 by Henry the Fowler (876-936). At the same time as re-establishing an effective central government, the greatest of the Saxon kings Otto I (called the Great, 912-973)

re-established the Empire by having himself crowned in Rome in 962. After marrying the widow of a Lombard king, Otto managed to extend his rule over most of Italy, and also took a great interest in artistic and cultural activities. Ottonian art was the result of the restoration of the Empire, and as such continued many of the traditions of Carolingian art while at the same time merging into what we know as the 'Romanesque.'

By the twelfth century western Europe had resumed the leadership of Christian civilization and the Crusades bore witness to its expansive force. At this time, Europe also saw the rise of national monarchies: in France, the Capetian dynasty began the unification of the country under the French crown with Louis VI (1108-1137), Louis VII (1137-1180) and Philip Augustus (1180-1223), whose Paris fortress was on the site now occupied by the Louvre. The two Louis were both fortunate to be assisted during their reigns by an astute politician and cleric, Abbot Suger (c.1081-1152). Suger imported goldsmiths from Lorraine in 1140 to work on the twenty-three foot high gold crucifix for the choir of Saint Denis and donated many treasures to the royal monastery which are now in the Louvre, including the eagle-shaped vase in Egyptian porphyry and silver gilt and the rock crystal vase set with precious gems, a gift from Eleanor of Aquitaine to Louis VII, who promptly handed it over to Suger. Other treasures subsequently confiscated during the French Revolution from Saint Denis, the Royal Wadrobe, the Order of St Esprit and the Ste Chapelle and placed in the Louvre include the ninth-century sword of the kings of France, sometimes called Charlemagne's Sword. This sacred sword of the Capetian, Valois and Bourbon kings of France is carried by Louis XIV in the famous royal portrait by Hyacinthe Rigaud.

Alongside the advent of national monarchies in France, in England (under Henry II in 1154) and in Spain, which had just undergone an arduous campaign of reconquest and whose symbol of national feeling was El Cid (d.1099), this period also witnessed the rise of urban communities in northern Italy in the early eleventh century. Self-governing communities like Venice, Genoa, Pisa and Lucca were soon to grow into independent states. In the north, communities and free cities supported by the power of the Hanseatic League in Flanders and Germany gave birth to a class of prosperous merchant patrons who could successfully compete with the most powerful of princes. With improvements in material life came the desire for increased knowledge. In Italy and Flanders from the twelfth century new public schools, independent of the Church, were founded using the vernacular (as opposed to Latin) for instruction. Universities were also founded at Bologna and Paris in 1120, in Padua in 1122 and in Naples in 1124.

Artistically Italy had continued to keep alive the techniques of panel painting, mosaic and fresco. While in France Abbot Suger had placed emphasis on the miraculous effects of stained glass, which was seen as the ideal medium for symbolic expression and made

Left A Carolingian ivory was reused to form this reliquary for the abbey of St Denis.

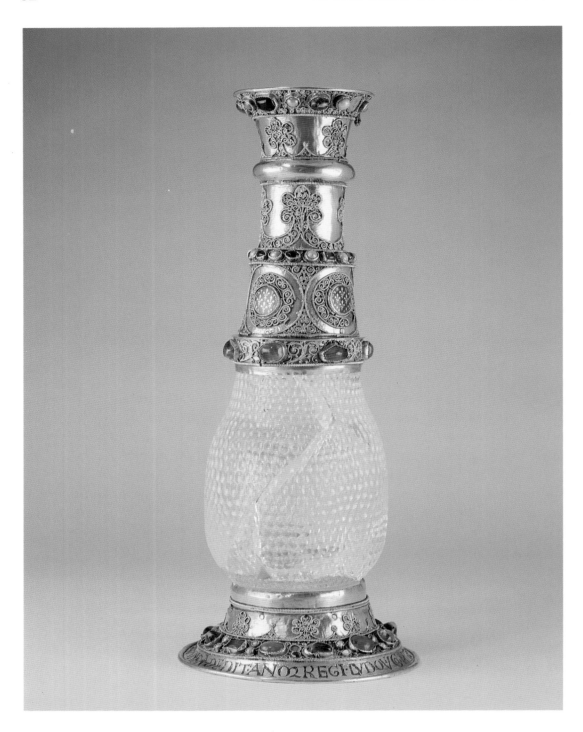

Left This twelfth-century vase, made of rock crystal set in silver gilt with gems, was given by Eleanor of Aquitaine to her first husband, Louis VII, who in turn presented it to the formidable and influential Abbot Suger.

Right St Francis of Assisi Receiving the Stigmata, usually attributed to the Florentine painter and architect Giotto di Bondone (c.1267-1337). Giotto is regarded as the founder of the central tradition of Western art, breaking away from Byzantine stylization and creating a convincing sense of pictorial space, but no surviving painting is firmly documented as by him.

stained glass the dominant pictorial art in northern Europe, in Italy a new wave of Byzantine influence developed in painting and lasted until the end of the thirteenth century. The interaction of this Byzantine influence with the Gothic style that sculptors and architects were assimilating produced a new style, the greatest exponent of which was the Florentine painter Giotto di Bondone (c.1267-1337). His main innovation was his ability to represent figures as solid forms arranged in three-dimensional space.

Simone Martini (c.1284-1344), who painted the little panel *Christ on the Way to Calvary* (c.1336-42) (originally part of a larger composition, a polyptych of the Passion that was used as a portable altar by travelling prelates), not only echoes his Sienese master Duccio in his use of bright colors and architectural details, but also betrays the influence of Giotto in his modelling of figures with their dramatic gestures and expressions. By the time Martini painted this panel, the so-called Middle Ages had given way to the revival of the arts and sciences of classical antiquity that we know as the 'Renaissance' (French for re-birth). One of the first masters of the Renaissance was the Italian poet

Petrarch, who embodied two salient features of the age, individualism and Humanism. A new self-awareness and self-assurance enabled Petrarch to claim that, compared to the enlightenment of antiquity, the 'Age of Faith' was really an era of darkness, and that pre-Christian antiquity represented the most enlightened stage of history. Humanism meant a belief in the importance of the humanities; learning in literature, history and philosophy in a secular rather than a religious framework. Having placed a conceptual barrier of a 'thousand years of darkness' between themselves and the ancients, Petrarch and his successors - unlike the medieval classicists – acknowledged that the Graeco-Roman world was dead and could be revived only in the mind by rediscovering ancient art and thoughts. The aim of the Renaissance was not to duplicate antique works but to equal or even surpass them, while at the same time attempting to reconcile classical philosophy with Christianity. To the Renaissance man the idea that pre-Christian or 'pagan' societies might also have been moral societies was quite possible.

The Louvre collection of Italian works from the fourteenth, and fifteenth centuries only really began

Above This Florentine altarpiece, *The Coronation of the Virgin*, is characteristic of the graceful, delicate work of the fifteenth-century painter Fra Angelico, who probably began his career as a manuscript illustrator.

with the establishment of the Musée Napoléon at the beginning of the nineteenth century. The early masters, or 'primitives' as they were called, had been neglected ever since the High Renaissance. The study of fourteenth- and fifteenth-century Italian, Flemish and German paintings began well before the study of their French contemporaries. While works by Van

Eyck and Fra Angelico were exhibited in the Musée Napoléon, works by French masters like the fifteenth-century painter Jean Fouquet were absent. Fouquet's works finally entered the national collection during the reign of Louis Philippe at the Château de Versailles, where the king was forming a *musée historique*; paintings were purchased as historical documents when the sitters were considered sufficiently interesting. Fouquet's portrait of Charles VII was bought as a 'Greek work,' implying that the authorities believed it to be Byzantine.

With regard to Italian works, artists earlier than

Perugino or Leonardo were absent from the royal collections. It was left to historians and connoisseurs like Seroux d'Agincourt and Artaud de Montor to pioneer a rediscovery. Works by Mantegna and Giovanni Bellini were in the first convoys brought from Italy in 1798 by Napoleon's army, and Vivant Denon went to Italy in 1811 to choose a series of Florentine altarpieces by Fra Angelico, Filippo Lippi, Ghirlandaio, Cimabue and Giotto. Following the operation of returning seized works of art to their countries of origin, this section of the museum remained surprisingly undisturbed.

The low regard in which the primitives were held is best indicated by the purchase price in 1834 of Simone Martini's *Christ on the Way to Calvary*: a mere 200 francs. Compare this with the 250,000 francs paid for a *Nativity* by the little known Umbrian painter Spagna. Other notable primitives entered the Louvre collection following the scandal and subsequent sale of the collection of the Marquis Campana. The director of a banking concern in Rome, the Marquis had accumulated a formidable collection of antiques and artworks by early masters that was financed by large sums of money 'borrowed' from his company. In 1857 the accounts were checked and the deficit revealed. Campana was arrested and sentenced to banishment and his collection offered for sale. After secret negotiations, the collection of 11,835 objects and 646 paintings was bought by Napoleon III. Unfortunately, this unique collection was scattered between various provincial museums, with the Louvre retaining only about one hundred Trecento and Quattrocento works. Among these masterpieces is Uccello's *The Battle of San Romano*, one of three panels representing the battle, a minor Florentine victory over the Sienese in 1432 (the other two are in the National Gallery, London, and the Uffizi Gallery, Florence). This used to be in the Palazzo Medici in Florence and is described by Vasari in his *Lives of the Artists*.

Above
The Barberini Ivory (central
section), Byzantine, early 6th
century
Ivory bas-relief 13½ × 10½ inches
(34.4 × 26.6 cm)

This ivory panel, which takes its
name from the family that once
owned it, is the central panel of a dip-
tych. It depicts an emperor on horse-
back – a classical Roman motif that remained popular in Byzantine art –
who is triumphing over his enemies.

The emperor has been identified in
turn as Justinian, Theodoric and Zeno
(who was a consul during Theodoric's reign), but the usual title accorded
it is 'Justinian, Defender of the Faith'.
At Justinian's ascension to the throne
the Byzantine world consisted of the

Balkan peninsula in Europe, Syria and Anatolia in Asia and Egypt in Africa. In his efforts to revive the Roman Empire, Justinian reconquered Africa from the Vandals, following his victory at Decium near Carthage (Tunisia). He took Spain and the Balearics from the Visigoths and Italy from the Ostrogoths at the Battle of Vesuvius in 523. It is not surprising therefore that the Barberini Ivory should be associated with Justinian.

Above
The Story of Jonah, third/fourth century AD
Incised gold sheet between two sheets of glass, 4¼ inches in diameter (10.7 cm)

According to the Bible, Jonah was thrown into the sea to calm the storm which God had set against him and was swallowed by a huge monster or whale, where he stayed for three days before being vomited up on a beach. In the view of the early Christians, this story prefigures the death and resurrection of Christ and of all Christian believers. This fragment of a ritual cup is concave in shape and depicts a Roman ship and the whale swallowing the Prophet, who appears to have fallen head first into the monster's mouth. Found in a cemetery in Rome, the fragment is inscribed at the top right 'Zesis', a Greek inscription frequently found on glassware of this type.

Above
Equestrian Statuette of Charlemagne, ninth century
Bronze, 9½ inches high (24 cm)

In the early Middle Ages, as a result of the decline of classical influence and the establishment of independent 'barbarian' kingdoms in Europe, sculpture was often reduced to linear rather than plastic ornamentation. Nevertheless, the antique was not completely forgotten, and the Holy Roman Emperor Charlemagne, leader of the Frankish kingdom and ally of the papacy, called for the revival of classical learning and art and created a center of patronage at the imperial court. His own equestrian statuette recalls earlier Roman models, but has in fact raised numerous questions as to its date and subject. Some believe it to date not from the Middle Ages but from the sixteenth century; others maintain that it is not a portrait of Charlemagne but of one of his successors.

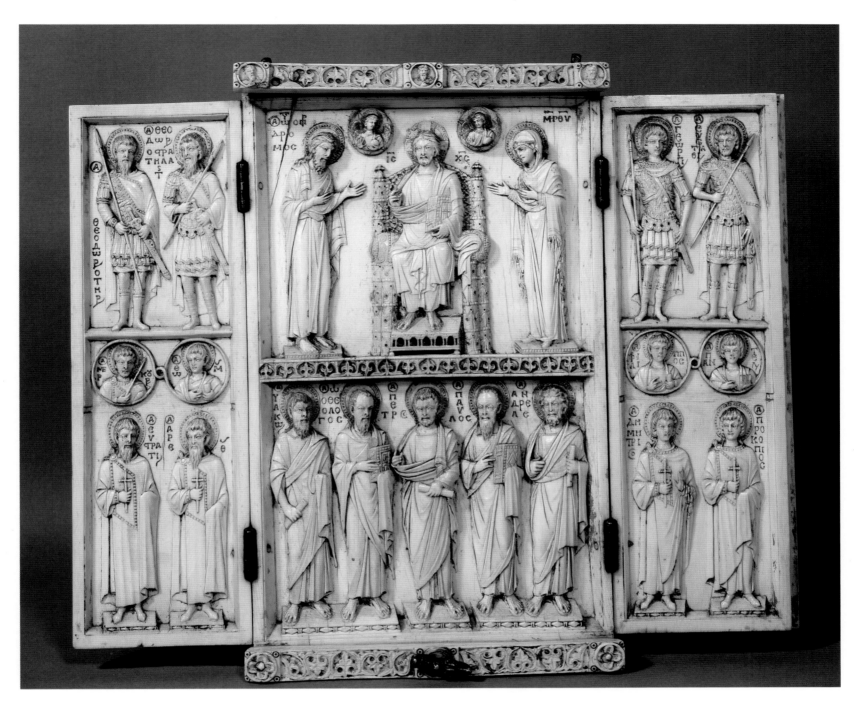

Left
The Sacred Sword of the Kings of France, ninth century (?) and fourteenth century
Gold, length of handle 8⅔ inches (22 cm)

This sword, sacred to the kings of France, has often been identified as the famous '*Joyeuse*': the sword of the first Holy Roman Emperor, Charlemagne (768-814), who was crowned by the Pope in Rome in 800 AD. It is possible that the handle dates from the Carolingian age, but there are certainly modifications from a later date.

Kept in the Abbey of Saint-Denis, the sword formed part of the collection of royal objects sacred to the Capet, Valois and Bourbon kings. In Rigaud's famous portrait of Louis XIV (page 130), the king carries the sword at his side, and it is also carried by Napoleon in David's coronation painting (page 142/3).

Above
The Harbaville Triptych,
tenth century
Ivory, central panel 9½ × 5½ inches (24 × 14 cm), side panels 8½ × 2¾ inches (21.5 × 7 cm)

The Harbaville Triptych, a Byzantine masterpiece, is a small portable altar which was in a collection in Arras before entering the Louvre. In the central panel, which is divided into two registers, Christ is depicted seated on a throne and flanked by the Virgin and St John. To either side of Christ's head, two angels in medallions hold the sun and the moon. In the lower register are five Apostles wearing classical togas. The side panels are symmetrical in composition: each carries two warriors in the upper register, while below are four saints, two in medallions and two full length.

The tenth century in Byzantine art, as exemplified by this fine ivory carving, was a period of great aesthetic achievement, comparable to the time of the Emperor Justinian and often called 'The Second Golden Age'.

Right
The Courajod Christ, French,
second quarter of the twelfth
century
Painted and gilded wood 61 inches high
(155 cm)

The *Courajod Christ* takes its name
from its donor, Louis Courajod (1841-
96) who gave the polychrome wood
sculpture to the Louvre in 1895.

While at first glance the overall
placement of the body may suggest a
Crucifixion, it is more likely that the
theme is one rarely treated by French
Romanesque sculptors, the Deposition or Descent from the Cross. The
body of Christ is treated with a slight
bend, while the right arm appears to
be dropping down and the head in-
clines forward and over the right
shoulder. This deliberate lack of symmetry reinforces the idea of Christ's
body being brought down from the
Cross.

Above
Vase in the Shape of an Eagle,
12th century
Porphyry and silver gilt, 17 inches high
(43.5 cm)

The dark purple body of this eagle-
shaped vase is fashioned from an
Egyptian porphyry vase. In contrast
the wings, head and tail are made of
silver gilt. The whole vase was
assembled in the twelfth century, an
outstanding example of the crafts-
manship of French Romanesque

metalworkers. This magnificent vase
was the gift of the powerful Abbot
Suger (adviser to King Louis XII) to
the monastery of St Denis.

The most important posts in the
medieval church were reserved for
members of the aristocracy; abbots
and bishops were not only of noble
birth but often wielded considerable
power because of their economic and
political interests. Not surprisingly,
the art that was created for monastic
use is just as lordly as secular pieces of
the same period.

Left
Ciborium of Alpais,
thirteenth century
Champlevé enamel, 12 inches high
(30.4 cm)

This ciborium, a covered vessel used for holding the Eucharist, bears the inscription on the interior of the cover: '*Magister G Alpais me fecit, Lemovicarum*' (Master G Alpais made me, Limoges).

Limoges in the thirteenth century was one of the most important centers for champlevé enamel work, but nothing is known about the identity of Master Alpais, since there are no other works signed by him. Limoges enamels and other fine-quality small portable works of art, such as embroideries and ivory carvings, played an important part in the diffusion of French Gothic art forms all over Europe. Originally from the Abbey of Montmajour, the ciborium became part of the Louvre collection in 1828.

Above
Crown of Saint Louis,
thirteenth century
Silver gilt and precious stones,
8¼ inches diameter (21 cm)

The Crown of Saint Louis, the pious King Louis IX of France (1226-1270), was made as a setting for the relics of Christ's Passion which Louis had bought from Baudouin, the Emperor of Constantinople and King of Jerusalem. In order to house such magnificent and valuable objects, Louis ordered the construction of what has been called the 'most beautiful reliquary ever built' – the Sainte Chapelle in Paris, consecrated in 1248.

This and other religious treasures were seized by the state during the Revolution and became part of the national collection later to be housed at the Louvre.

Right
Christ on the Way to Calvary,
c.1339–1344?
Martini, Simone, c.1284–1344
Panel, 10 × 21¾ inches (30 × 20 cm)

This small panel, by one of the most distinguished painters of the Sienese school, was originally part of a larger composition which was divided up in 1826. Two panels representing the *Annunciation* and the panels of the *Deposition* and the *Crucifixion* passed into the Van Ertborn collection and were eventually bequeathed to the museum in Antwerp. The panel of the *Entombment* went to Berlin in 1901, while the Louvre panel was purchased from M L Saint Denis in 1834. On the frames of the panels of the *Crucifixion* and *Deposition* are the words *Symon Pinxit* (Simon painted this).

This polyptych of the Passion was one of the small portable altars which travelling clerics used. In the *Deposition* panel, the prelate himself is shown kneeling. The Louvre panel bears on the reverse the arms of the Orsini family, a member of which might have commissioned the work, since several of the Orsini had links with the papal court at Avignon and the Angevin court at Naples. The panel may have been painted at Avignon between 1339 and 1344, but some experts believe it was painted in Italy before this period and came into France much later.

Above
Madonna and Child with Angels,
c.1300?
Cimabue (Cenno di Peppi), active 1240–1302
Panel, 13ft 9 inches × 9ft ½ inches (427 × 280 cm)

This huge altarpiece by the Florentine painter Cimabue, precursor of Giotto, was formerly in the Church of San Francesco in Pisa and was selected in 1811 by Baron Vivant-Denon, the Director of the Musée Napoléon, to form part of a new collection of Italian 'primitives'. The painting was among the property of the suppressed religious houses of Tuscany. Exhibited at the Louvre in 1814, the painting remained in France, after the Florentine commission charged with reclaiming seized works left it in the Louvre's possession. It is related to two other large thirteenth-century Florentine altarpieces: *The Madonna of Santa Trinita* (Uffizi Gallery) and the *Rucellai Madonna* (Santa Maria Novella) which, according to Vasari, were all painted by Cimabue. The modern view is that the Uffizi Madonna is by Cimabue, the Rucellai by Duccio.

Here Cimabue has depicted the Madonna enthroned, but seated on a structure that represents the Church itself. While there is evidence of a new spirit in the perspectival treatment of the throne, the image nevertheless retains the frontality of medieval art.

Left
Reliquary Arm of Saint Louis of Toulouse, 1337
Rock crystal, silver, silver gilt and enamel, 23½ inches high (60 cm)

At one time, the rock crystal receptacle of this Italian-made reliquary contained the arm bone of Saint Louis of Toulouse. The reliquary is also decorated with the armorial bearings of France and the houses of Anjou and Aragon. Toward the end of the Middle Ages, reliquaries of various shapes and sizes were part of the cult surrounding individual saints. Many of the holy relics they contained were believed to have magical or healing powers. In Italy, Saint Louis of Toulouse was the patron saint of the Guelf faction, and here the reliquary adopts the form of the relic it contained. Formerly in the Spitzer collection, this piece became part of the Louvre collection in 1891.

Right
A Princess of the House of Este, c.1433
Pisanello (Antonio di Puccio Pisano), c.1380–1455
Panel, 17 × 11¾ inches (43 × 30 cm)

Pisanello is one of the foremost exponents of the International Gothic style in Italian painting. While there is no doubt as to the painter of this profile portrait, the identity of the sitter remains a mystery. The most convincing theory is based on the embroidery on the sleeve of the woman's dress, representing the two-handled vase of the d'Este family. This device is also to be found on the medal which Pisanello designed for Lionello d'Este. Marguerite of Gonzaga (d.1439) is one candidate; she was the wife of Lionello and the picture could well date from the time of their marriage in 1433. A second possibility is that it is the portrait of Genevra d'Este – the sprig of juniper on her shoulder could be a visual pun on her name. Genevra was poisoned by her husband Sigismondo Pandolfo Malatesta when she was only 22. Whoever she is, she is a young woman, hardly more than a girl, wearing the fashionable hairstyle of the period, where the hairs on the brow were plucked out and the rest drawn back from the face.

The Madonna of Chancellor Rolin, c. 1436
Van Eyck, Jan, c.1390–1441
Oil on panel, 26 × 24½ inches
(66 × 62 cm)

Van Eyck's picture of the Virgin presenting the infant Christ to the donor, Chancellor Rolin, is full of symbolic meaning expressed through the minute details in the representation of appearances. The Virgin is shown as the Queen of Heaven being crowned by an attendant angel. The scene takes place in a Romanesque 'loggia', the sculptured capitals of which are carved with themes from the Christmas cycle, and which stands for the Temple of Jerusalem. Beyond is a small enclosed garden, symbolic of the Virgin's purity, and the town in the background represents Jerusalem. The actual identity of the town has been the cause of much speculation: Bruges, Lyons, Liege, Geneva, London, Autun and Prague have all been suggested.

The donor is traditionally believed to be Nicolas Rolin, Chancellor of Burgundy (1376?–1462) at the court of Duke Philip the Good. In 1425 Van Eyck entered the Duke's household and the painting is believed to be from around 1436. This date is based on the evidence of Rolin's apparent age and on certain stylistic affinities which link this work with the *Madonna with Canon van der Paele* altarpiece which bears the date 1436.

Originally in the collegiate church of Autun, in Burgundy, this painting was confiscated during the Revolution and sent to the Louvre in 1800.

Portrait of Charles VII, King of France, c. 1444
Fouquet, Jean, d. between 1477 and 1481
Panel, 34 × 28½ inches (86 × 72 cm)

This painting still retains its original frame, on which appears the following inscription: '*Le très victorieux roi de France Charles septiesme de ce nom*' (the most victorious king of France

Charles, seventh of that name). The inscription suggests that the portrait may have been painted after the truce at Arras in 1444, or after the 1450 Treaty of Formigny. Stylistically the earlier date is favored by art historians; by 1447 Fouquet had visited Italy and painted a portrait of Pope Eugene IV (who died that year) but the painting betrays no trace of any Renaissance influence, remaining essentially

formal, sculptural and Gothic in spirit.

A watercolor copy, now in the Bibliothèque Nationale, which was made when the painting was housed in the Sainte Chapelle at Bourges (destroyed in 1757), revealed that originally this painting did not have a brown-checked pattern on a green background. In 1939 this later and somewhat clumsy addition was removed, although traces remain.

The Battle of San Romano, c.1455
Uccello (Paolo di Dono),
1397–1475
Panel, 71 × 125½ inches (180 × 316 cm)

This picture, by one of the most distinctive painters of the early Renaissance, is part of a painting in three panels, representing the battle of San Romano, which used to be in the Palazzo Medici in Florence. Two of the panels were sold in the 19th century. The National Gallery, London, has one panel, the Louvre acquired its panel with the Campana collection in 1864, while the third remained in the Uffizi Gallery, Florence. Attachments to the top of each of these panels suggest that they may have been placed at an angle at the top of Lorenzo il Magnifico's

room where they formed part of the decorative scheme. San Romano was a minor victory by the Florentines over the Sienese in June 1432. Commanded by Niccolo da Tolentino, the Florentines had held out for eight hours after a surprise attack by the Sienese. The tide turned in their favor following the arrival of reinforcements led by Michelotto da Cotignola. The Louvre panel represents the counter-attack led by Cotignola, who is shown enouraging his troops across the Arno.

The Crucifixion, 1457–59
Mantegna, Andrea, 1431–1506
Panel, 29½ × 37½ inches (76 × 96 cm)

This panel is the central part of the
'predella' or subsidiary portion of a
large altarpiece painted between 1457
and 1459 for the high altar of the
church of San Zeno in Verona. It was
commissioned by the abbot of the
monastery, Gregorio Correr. The
altarpiece was brought to the Louvre
in 1798 and exhibited. In 1806 two of
the predella panels (*Mount of Olives*
and *The Resurrection*) were sent to the
museum in Tours. Later, in 1815, the
central panel and the two wings of the
altarpiece were returned to Italy, following the commission of that year to
reclaim works seized by Napoleon
from the Veneto, but two of the predella panels stayed in the Tours
museum and this central predella
panel remained in the Louvre.

The Crucifixion formed the exact
center of the predella. The foreground
figures, cut by the frame, help to in-
crease the effect of perspectival reces-
sion, while the accurate depiction of
the Roman soldiers' arms are evidence
both of Mantegna's understanding of
the aesthetic qualities of the antique
and his concern with historical accuracy. The towns of the Veneto were in
fact the chief centers for the traffic in
antiquities from the early 14th
century, some time before Florence
started to establish *cabinets d'antiquités*.

The Braque Triptych, c. 1461?
Van der Weyden, Rogier,
c.1400–64
left panel: *Saint John the Baptist (left)*
16¼ × 13½ inches (41 × 34.4 cm)
central panel: *Christ the Redeemer between
the Virgin and St John the Evangelist
(above)* 16⅛ × 27⅛ inches (41 × 69 cm)
right panel: *Saint Mary Magdalen (right)*
16¼ × 13½ (41 × 34.4 cm)

On the back of this portable triptych
are the armorial bearings of Jehan
Braque and his wife, Catherine de
Brabant, of Tournai, who were married in c. 1450-51. Jehan Braque died
soon afterwards (in 1452) and his
widow, who did not remarry until
1461, may have commissioned this
triptych in his memory. The central
panel represents Christ in benedic-
tion; the right panel depicts Saint
Mary Magdalen, and the left Saint
John the Baptist. On the back of the
left-hand shutter is a skull on a broken
brick, the Braque coat of arms, and
the inscription: '*Mirez-vous si orgueil-
leux et avers, mon corps fu beaux ore est
viande a (vers).*' The skull, a traditional
device for a *memento mori*, coupled
with these lines, no doubt refers to
Jehan's death.

Left
**Portrait of Francesco Sassetti
(Portrait of an Old Man and His
Grandson)** c.1480
Ghirlandaio, Domenico (1449–94)
Tempera and oil on panel, 24⅜ × 18⅛
inches (62 × 46 cm)

Ghirlandaio was a pupil of Alessio
Baldovinetti and master to Michelangelo, and was known in Florence as a
painter gifted for his observation of
details. He transformed many of his
religious paintings, such as the frescoes for Santa Trinita and the choir of
Santa Maria Novella, into scenes of
daily life featuring portraits of prominent Florentine personalities.

Here the disfigured face of an old
man is transformed by the smile he
directs to his grandson, who returns
his look with affection. Depth is given
to the composition by the addition of
the open window, through which a
stylized landscape is visible. Furthermore, the window frame serves to
counter the sharp oblique line created
by the two figures.

Above
**Virgin and Child Surrounded by
Angels**, mid-fifteenth century
Duccio, Agostino di, 1418–1481
Marble 31¾ × 27½ inches (81 × 77 cm)

This bas-relief by the Florentine
master Duccio was removed from
Italy at the beginning of the nineteenth century by General de Bonnières, one of Napoleon's officers
during the First Empire. Bonnières
took the relief back to France, where
he had it installed in his own chateau
at Auvilliers in the valley of the Oise.
Later the sculpture was transferred to
a local church, and finally entered the
Louvre collection in 1903. This bas-
relief is typical of Duccio's work; the
treatment of the faces and the elegant
handling of the draperies and hair are
hallmarks of his style.

Botticelli, Sandro (Alessandro di
Mariano Filipepi) c. 1445–1510
Oil on canvas, 28½ × 19⅛ inches
(73 × 49 cm)

Botticelli, who is believed to have
trained under the Florentine painter
Filippo Lippi, was called to Rome by
the Pope in 1481 to assist in the decorations of the Sistine Chapel. Nevertheless, almost all his other work was
done in Florence, where Botticelli
was working under the patronage of
the Medici family. It was for Lorenzo
de Pierfrancesco dei Medici that Botticelli painted his best known works,
The Primavera and *The Birth of Venus*,
which reveal the influence of the
Humanist philosophy popular with
the Medicis. In this painting of a
Madonna, however, Botticelli continues the long-established tradition
of painting images of the Virgin and
Child.

Above
**Portrait of a Man (Il
Condottiere)**, 1475
Messina, Antonello da, c.1430
Oil on panel, 13¾ × 11 inches
(35 × 28 cm)

Born in Sicily, Messina probably
acquired his knowledge of northern
techniques, including that of painting
in oil, from his contacts with northern
European artists, in particular Petrus
Christus, who were artistically dominant in Naples at this time. Indeed
Messina is usually credited with in-
troducing the skill to Italy. The effects
that can be achieved in oils are very
different to those from tempera,
where the pigment is bound with egg.
Tempera produces a much 'flatter'
look; its effect is derived from areas of
flat color, while oils, which can be
built up in layers of pigment and
glazes, can lend itself to greater 'realism'. In technique, Messina's portrait
betrays the influence of Van Eyck, yet
in his analysis of his sitter's face, with
its clenched jaws and stern expression, Messina's approach is unmistak-
ably Italian. In the manner of northern
artists, there is an inscription at the
bottom of the picture which reads:
'1475. *Antonellus Messineus me pinxit.*'
(Antonello da Messina painted me).

Left

Self-Portrait, 1493
Dürer, Albrecht, 1471–1528
Parchment pasted on canvas, 22¼ ×
17½ inches (56.5 × 44.5 cm)

The date and the plant in the artist's hand suggest to many historians that this is a betrothal portrait (*Brautportrat*). Dürer has depicted himself holding a flower spray which has been identified by botanists as *eryngium*

amethystinum, the German name of which is '*Mannestreue*', meaning conjugal fidelity; it is considered to have aphrodisiac qualities. In 1493 Dürer was 22 years old and, having completed his apprenticeship, he married

Agnes Frey. The lines written beside the date at the top of the picture reveal both the Christian outlook and philosophical temperament of the artist and the intention of the painting:

Myj sach die gat
Als es oben schtat

(My affairs follow the course that destiny has allotted me). Thus the groom puts his future life into the hands of God.

Above
The Moneylender and His Wife, 1514
Metsys, Quentin, 1465/6-1530
Oil on panel, 28 × 27 inches
(70 × 67 cm)

This painting is very reminiscent of fifteenth-century work, that of Van Eyck in particular, with its naturalistic detail and the reflection in the convex mirror, a device similar to that Van Eyck used in the *Arnolfini Marriage* in the National Gallery, London. In fact Van Eyck is known to have painted 'a merchant at his accounts, with an assistant, the figure half length' in 1440. The Flemish Metsys is

believed to have followed Van Eyck very closely in this painting of a merchant, here a jeweler, counting his gold with his wife at his side. She has paused in her perusal of a Book of Hours, fascinated by the gold; the open book shows the figure of the Virgin. An inscription on the original frame (fortunately recorded before the frame was lost) made clear the message and moral of the work: it was a passage from the Bible (*Leviticus* XIX.36), '*Satura justa et aequa sint pondera*' (just balances, just weights, shall ye have).

On the roll of parchment resting on the book on the shelf is inscribed: 'Quinten Matsys, *Schilder* 1514'.

CHAPTER THREE

High Renaissance and Baroque

In the sixteenth century, a period generally referred to as the High Renaissance, great masters such as Leonardo, Raphael, Titian and Michelangelo were regarded as men of genius who far outstripped and overshadowed the achievements of their predecessors. These artists were fêted and acclaimed in their own day; Leonardo, according to popular mythology, died in the arms of the French king Francis I, while Titian was made a Count Palatine by the Holy Roman Emperor Charles V. Their lasting influence was such that the High Renaissance is often viewed as an 'artistic turning point' and all artists before Raphael referred to as 'primitives.'

The problem with labels such as 'High Renaissance' is that they imply a single clearly identifiable style in art. While there are discernible stylistic differences between works from the Early and High Renaissance in Florence and Rome, the distinction in Venetian art is far less clear-cut. A further complication is the question of what happened after the High Renaissance. Most of the outstanding works of the period were produced between around 1495 and 1520 but, of our famous personalities, only Michaelangelo and Titian lived beyond 1520. There is, therefore, a period of some 75 years between the end of the High Renaissance in Europe and the beginning of the stylistic period known as the Baroque. Once again in this intermediary period there is no single style, but the most frequently discussed trend in art at the time is that of 'Mannerism.'

Even today the scope and meaning of the term mannerism is problematic. The original meaning was somewhat derogatory, designating a particular group of artists in Florence and Rome whose 'artificial' style was derived in part from Raphael and Michelangelo. More recently, Mannerist works have been seen as part of a wider movement in art that denied the established authority of 'nature' and the 'ancients' and replaced these with what has been called an 'inner vision.'

At the same time, most sixteenth-century artists north of the Alps were indifferent to the achievements of the High Renaissance. Instead of Tuscany, Flanders was to provide leadership in northern art. By 1500, the so-called 'Late Gothic' painting of the north's period of isolation is over-run by a new northern Renaissance. Yet even here there is a great diversity of trends, due in part to the various regional differences displayed by Florentine, Venetian and Roman art.

The term 'Baroque' has been used now for more than a century to designate the style of art in the period between 1600 and 1750. Its original meaning of 'irregular,' 'contorted' and even 'grotesque' is now largely forgotten. The exception to this is the designation of mishapen pearls as 'baroque.' There is general agreement that the Baroque style developed in Rome around 1600, but the impulse behind it remains in dispute. While some claim that the Baroque expressed the spirit of the Counter-Reformation and was supported by the princes of the Church, the style nevertheless penetrated into the Protestant north very quickly. It was favored by the absolute monarchy in France (in fact many French are reluctant to use the term Baroque and instead prefer to call it the 'Louis XIV' style), but also flourished in bourgeois Holland. In short, like the works produced in the High Renaissance, Baroque art appears in many guises, from the subdued classicism of officially sponsored state art under Louis XIV to the dramatically lit effects and subjects produced particularly by the Bolognese painters and the intimate genre scenes and interiors of Dutch painters.

The collection of French sixteenth-century paintings in the Louvre is a comparatively recent one; the outstanding exception is the *Portrait of Francis I* attributed to Jean Clouet, which has been part of the national collection ever since it was commissioned in around 1530. It is possible that the royal collection had many such portraits, since Bailly's inventory in 1710 mentions 251 small portraits of past kings and nobles. All that remains in the Louvre of this collection is a full-length depiction of Henry II, which is a studio copy of a painting housed in the Uffizi Gallery in Florence.

There is, however, an enormous collection of prints and drawings (which also contains some small portraits) from the sixteenth century, which was bequeathed by Roger de Gaignière on his death in 1716. Other works from this period passed during the Revolution into the Musée des Monuments Français and

Left François Clouet: *Pierre Quthe.* Clouet's father Jean (d.1540) was also a noted painter, responsible for the famous portrait of Francis I; François' work is more Italianate in style.

entered the Louvre in 1817, while twentieth-century purchases have included Clouet's portrait of *Pierre Quthe*, Corneille de Lyon's *Pierre Aymeric* and the anonymous *Portrait of a Couple* by a French artist.

The Louvre's collection of Italian High Renaissance works of art is undoubtedly one of its greatest treasures and certainly one of the finest outside Italy itself. The foundations of this collection were laid by Francis I, whose intention it was to invite to France the most 'modern' artists of the time. Having succeeded in attracting the most famous of these, Leonardo da Vinci, in 1516, Francis provided the artist with a state pension and installed him in a pleasant house at Cloux near Amboise. Here Leonardo, although too ill to paint, advised the French king on engineering and architectural projects as well as devising masques and other entertainments. He had brought some of his works with him from Italy and on October 10th, 1517 he showed three paintings to the Cardinal of Aragon who was visiting him. The Cardinal's secretary, Antonio de Beatis, has provided us with an account of the meeting and noted that the three paintings Leonardo showed were a 'Saint John the Baptist,' a 'Saint Anne' and a 'Portrait of a Lady' which is almost certainly the *Mona Lisa*. It is possible that Francis purchased these paintings (and maybe others including the *Bacchus* and the *Belle Feronière*) after Leonardo's death on May 2nd, 1519 from Francesco Melzi, Leonardo's executor, although how exactly these works entered the royal collection is still a mystery. We do know that the first work by Leonardo to be seen in France was a painting depicting the *Virgin with a Spindle*, bought by the French Secretary of State Florimund Robertet and now lost. Evidently this painting met with such enthusiasm at the court that it encouraged the then king, Louis XII, to persist in his own efforts to lure Leonardo to France. In 1507, when Louis XII entered Milan in triumph, it was Leonardo who designed the festivities in his honor at the Castello Sforzesco and it is believed that Louis brought back from Milan Leonardo's *The Virgin of the Rocks*. By whatever route these paintings entered the collection, they are certainly the most famous and probably the most valuable items in the Louvre.

Leonardo was not the only Florentine artist working in France: in 1518 Francis I summoned to the French court Andrea del Sarto, who painted *Charity* during his stay. Francis already owned two works by del Sarto, a *Madonna* and *The Holy Family*. Furthermore, Rosso Fiorentino was employed to work on the decorations for the royal residence at Fontainebleau. It was also for Francis I that Raphael painted *St Michael Confounding the Devil* and *The Holy Family*, both diplomatic gifts presented to the king by Lorenzo II de Medici, Duke of Urbino, acting on behalf of Pope Leo X. Among other important works collected by the king were Raphael's

Left Leonardo da Vinci: *The Virgin of the Rocks*, which may have been acquired by Louis XII during his trip to Milan in 1507.

La Belle Jardinière and *Portrait of the Artist with a Friend*. The *Portrait of Joan of Aragon*, on which it is believed Raphael collaborated with Giulio Romano, was probably a gift to the king from Cardinal Bibiena.

Francis I was particularly attracted by the artists of Florence and Rome, cities with which he had strong diplomatic relations. On the whole Venetian art was disregarded since the Republic was more closely allied with the Holy Roman Emperor. Within Francis' collection there was a single Venetian work by the great master Titian. This was a profile portrait of the king, painted in 1538 after a medallion made by Benvenuto Cellini; there was no contact between the royal sitter and the Venetian artist.

It is believed that Francis' collection also contained works by contemporary Flemish artists. We know, for example, that Joos van Cleve came from Antwerp to Fontainebleau in 1530 to paint portraits of the king and the royal family, but not a single example remained in the collection. Lebrun's inventory in 1618 records only a handful of Flemish paintings from the late fifteenth and early sixteenth centuries.

The basis of the royal collection, kept for a long time at Fontainebleau and only later transferred to the Louvre, was considerably enlarged by Louis XIV, who sought to form a collection that would in its magnificence reflect the brilliance and opulence of his reign. Many of the superb paintings he accumulated entered the collection from two sources: the acquisition of part of Cardinal Mazarin's collection in 1661, and that of the banker and collector Everhard Jarbach between 1662 and 1671. These acquisitions included Correggio's *Antiope, Saint Catherine* and the *Allegories*; Raphael's *Portrait of Castiglione, Saint George* and *Saint Michael*; Titian's *Pardo Venus, The Supper at Emmaus* and the *Man with a Glove*; as well as paintings by Veronese and Giulio Romano. Many of these had been bought in London in about 1650 when the English king Charles I's famous collection of art was dispersed, following his arrest and execution. Charles' collection at the beginning of the seventeenth century had been the finest in Europe. Many of the Italian works had come from the Gonzaga family collection in Mantua, which the king had bought in its entirety in 1627.

Other Italian Renaissance works were introduced to Louis XIV's collection: works by Agnolo Bronzino, Jacopo Pontormo, a series of paintings by Jacopo Bassano which was to decorate the rooms of the Grand Apartments at Versailles, and Veronese's vast work *Feast at the House of Simon*, which was a diplomatic gift to the king from the Venetian Republic and was later incorporated by Louis XV into the decorative scheme for the Salon d'Hercule at Versailles.

The Louvre collection of Italian Renaissance works was greatly enlarged during the Revolution and the Empire, only to have many of the masterpieces returned to their countries of origin in 1815. Only a handful of works remained, among them paintings by Titian and Tintoretto. On the whole, the Italian works that entered the Louvre during the Revolution and remained there were works that had been in France for some time. Paintings by Mantegna and Perugino had formed part of Isabella d'Este's collection seized in 1801 from the Château de Richelieu, while other important works with religious subjects, such as those by Fiorentino and Bartolomeo, were removed from the cathedral of Autun and various provincial chapels.

The Louvre's collection of Flemish art from both the fifteenth and sixteenth centuries is once again due to the exploits of Napoleon Bonaparte. The Musée Napoléon included in its collection several panels of the magnificent *Altarpiece of the Mystic Lamb* by the Van Eyck brothers, which had been removed from Ghent, the outstanding *Virgin of Canon van der Paele*, also removed from Ghent, and Memling's triptych of *The Last Judgment* and *Saint Catherine*, taken as booty from Brussels. While all these works were returned to their homes in 1816, the Louvre was fortunate in retaining both Rogier van der Weyden's *The Annunciation* (taken from Turin) and the magnificent *Madonna of Chancellor Rolin* by Jan van Eyck, taken from the collegiate church at Autun.

Another notable acquisition, although this time a legitimate purchase, was that of Quentin Metsys' painting *The Banker and His Wife*, made in Paris in 1806. This and several other works were purchased during the Restoration and the July Monarchy. In the period 1845 to 1873 the Louvre received a series of gifts and made a number of purchases of important Flemish and Dutch works from the sixteenth century, including van der Weyden's *Braque Triptych* and Hieronymus Bosch's *Ship of Fools*, which was donated by the former keeper of the Louvre, Camille Benoit, in 1918.

The history of the Louvre's collection of seventeenth-century works of art not only illustrates the changing patterns of taste in France but also clearly reflects the way in which this period in art has been valued. The seventeenth-century collection was formed very gradually, with the first pieces of the collection reflecting the tastes of the monarchy. Later contributions demonstrate the importance given to this period by art historians.

Louis XIII had acquired a few works, generally in the form of vast pictorial schemes for decorations for his various châteaux. It was Louis XIV who formed the magnificent collection of French art from the seventeenth century, which is essentially 'classical' in taste. In fact Louis XIV's collection chiefly consisted of works by three French artists working in Rome, Nicolas Poussin, Claude Lorrain and Moïse Valentin; these were the only ones the king considered worthy enough to hang alongside the Italian masters of the sixteenth and seventeenth centuries. In addition Louis naturally included works by his own official artists, Lebrun and later Pierre Mignard. Of the 38 Poussins in the Louvre, 31 belonged originally to the king. In addition, Louis owned ten Claudes and nearly all Lebrun's work, the exceptions being those Lebrun painted for religious institutions which were seized during the Revolution.

Louis XV continued to make purchases that would have pleased his grandfather. Poussin's *Saint Francis Xavier* was bought from the Jesuits in 1763 when the king suppressed their order, and two further works by Valentin were bought from the estate of the Prince de Carignan in 1742.

In contrast, Louis XVI enjoyed a different aspect of seventeenth-century art. Having inherited his ancestor's collection of 'Roman' or classically inspired works, the king, with advice and assistance from the Comte d'Angivillier, concentrated on 'Parisian' works, which were considered more restrained and refined. Particularly popular were the works of Eustache le Sueur. Further 'Parisian' paintings entered the Louvre during the Revolution, most of them seized from the nobility, including d'Angivillier himself. Additional confiscations from churches and convents constituted the greater part of the collection. Despite this great influx of works from the seventeenth century, purchases of French art of this period continued to be made up until the nineteenth century. During the first half of the nineteenth century, the pace of contributions to the collection slowed down. In 1869, however, the superb collection amassed by Dr La Caze entered the Louvre and the museum was now provided with the finest collection of French seventeenth-century works.

The first Flemish works from this period in the royal collection were by living artists who had been summoned to Paris by the Queen Mother, Marie de' Medici. Peter Paul Rubens was commissioned by Marie to paint the decorations for the Long Gallery of the Palais du Luxembourg, which was inaugurated in 1625 for the marriage of Henrietta Maria of France and Charles I of England. Rubens painted a vast cycle of 24 canvases illustrating and, naturally, glorifying the life of Marie de' Medici from her birth in Florence to her reconciliation with her son Louis XIII. Historical facts and the occasional imaginary event are transformed into an allegory representing the finest achievement in Baroque painting. Though popular with the Italian-born queen, Rubens' work does not seem to have appealed to general Parisian taste in the mid-century, when a more sober classicism was favored. It was not until the 1660s that Flemish works were once more to enter the royal collection. These were in part acquired from Mazarin's estate, but it was Jarbach's collection which provided the masterpieces by Rubens and Van Dyck.

Most of the seventeenth-century Flemish works now in the Louvre were again originally owned by the French nobility, in particular the Duc d'Orléans and the Prince de Carignan. The Comte d'Angivillier made purchases of Flemish works a major feature of his program of acquisition for the royal collection, which bought works directly from collectors, dealers or public sales. The Louvre collection was further in-

Right Van Dyck: *Charles I.* Part of the English king's collection came to rest in the Louvre after his execution.

Above Rembrandt: *Self-Portrait as an Old Man*.

creased during the Revolution, particularly in the area of genre paintings and small-format pieces such as still lifes. The vast majority of Flemish works in the Louvre, however, are there thanks to the generosity of private individuals. The La Caze bequest included more than 70 Flemish pieces, while the twentieth-century bequests by Victor Bouquet, Carlos de Beiste-gui and the Rothschild family have provided the Louvre with further masterpieces of Flemish art.

Paradoxically, while Flemish art was admired and collected, the Dutch masters were for a long time over-looked. This is due in part to the high status accorded by the official Académie Royale to 'history paintings.'

The Dutch painters were largely concerned with representing scenes from everyday life, such as interiors, genre scenes and still lifes, which were considered by the Académie to be 'inferior' subjects. The greatest Dutch master, Rembrandt, was largely unknown in France during his lifetime. It seems that many French were shocked by the Dutchman's technique: the art critic and architect Félicien des Araux described his work as like a 'rough sketch.' Others were outraged by an apparent display of 'bad taste.' The diplomatic gift of a series of *Views of Brazil* by Frans Post from Maurice of Nassau to the French king was not considered so much a work of art as an exotic 'document,' and was duly consigned to the Cabinet des Curiosités.

The first indication of a change of outlook came in 1671 when Rembrandt's *Portrait of the Artist* was purchased. This was followed by the purchase of several works by Rembrandt's pupil Gerrit Dou between 1684 and 1715. From then on French collectors, already enamored of Flemish art, began the systematic acquisition of Dutch landscapes, still lifes, genre scenes and portraits, in which they now discovered a certain 'truth to life' alongside a delicate technique and interesting lighting effects.

In 1742 the royal collection was enriched by several fine Dutch works acquired from the estate of the Prince de Carignan, including Rembrandt's *The Angel Raphael leaving Tobias*. But it was under Louis XVI that the most important purchases of Dutch art were made, again either through private dealers or from the public sales of collections such as that of Randon de Boisset in 1777 and the Comte de Vaudreuil in 1784, which both provided the Louvre with several works by Rembrandt and Jacob van Ruisdael.

The Parisians' new infatuation with Dutch art is best exemplified by the lists of works seized from the emigrés during the Revolution: Rembrandt's *The Supper at Emmaus* and two self-portraits; Abraham Bloemaert's *Adoration* and Gerard Ter Borch's *The Concert* are just a few among hundreds of master works.

The nineteenth-century appreciation of Dutch masters was widespread, particularly among contemporary French artists like Théodore Rousseau, Gustave Courbet, Edouard Manet and Odilon Redon. In the second half of the nineteenth and the early twentieth centuries the Louvre benefitted from the collections created in response to the recent interest in seventeenth-century Dutch art in the form of the generous La Caze bequest, the Schlichting bequest in 1914, the bequest by the Comte de l'Espine in 1930, the Nicolas bequest in 1948, and works originally from the collection of Baron Alphonse de Rothschild presented in 1974 by Madame Piatigorsky.

The seventeenth-century Italian works in the Louvre again owe their existence to Louis XIV. While a few 'modern' works had already entered the royal collection under Louis XIII, it was the dispersal of the Mazarin and Jarbach collections which formed the basis of Louis XIV's collection of major seventeenth-century Italian works, among them Caravaggio's *Death of the Virgin* and Guido Reni's *The Story of Hercules*. Later gifts and purchases from Italian and French connoisseurs, including Charles Le Nôtre who designed the kings' gardens, added works by the Carracci brothers, Il Guercino, Domenichino and Albani.

Under Louis XV, purchases from the estate of the Prince de Carignan introduced works by Pietro da Cortona and Giovanni Castiglione, while under Louis XVI the Comte d'Angivillier made careful and systematic purchases with a view to making the future museum comprehensive in this department.

While many of the seventeenth-century works from Bologna had a very short life in the Musée Napoléon, some, such as work by Ludovico and Annibale Carracci's *The Virgin Appears to St Hyacinth* and *The Virgin Appears to St Luke and St Catherine* remained in Paris as part of the Emilian collection, which was later transferred to the Louvre and which is believed by many to be the finest and most complete collection outside of Bologna itself.

Left
The Ship of Fools c.1500
Bosch, Hieronymus, 1450?-1516?
Tempera and oil on panel, 22 × 12⅝
inches (58 × 32 cm)

Bosch was born and lived at 's-Herto-
genbosch (from which he derived his
surname), a commercial center which
stood somewhat apart from other
Flemish cities where great art was
flourishing. Bosch was less interested
in the traditional subjects of European
painting than in satirical themes and
popular proverbs. *The Ship of Fools*
was inspired by Sebastian Brandt's
book *Das Narrenschiff*, published in
Basle in 1494. This tells of a voyage to
the Isle of Folly, Narragonia, by men
who are given to vice. The mysticism
of the Middle Ages had, by this time,
given way to a moralizing attitude.
Later editions of Brandt's book,
which were decorated with engravings, were extremely popular and
they may have served as the basis for
Bosch's painting.

Right
Apollo and Marsyas, c.1500
Perugino, Pietro (Pietro Vanucci)
1446-1523
Oil on canvas, 15¼ × 11¼ inches
(39 × 29 cm)

Perugino is believed to have been a
pupil of Piero della Francesca and it is
possible that he was also later an assistant to Andrea del Verrocchio, who
was also Leonardo's master in
Florence. Perugino is particularly
known for his rendering of space and
atmospheric perspective.

In this work Perugino recalls the
legend of Marsyas, a Phrygian satyr in
Greek mythology, who found the
flute that Athena discarded because it
distorted her face when she played it.
Marsyas challenged the god Apollo to
a musical contest on condition that the
winner could do what he pleased with
the vanquished. The Muses judged
Apollo the winner, who thereupon
bound Marsyas to a tree and flayed
him alive.

Left
Mona Lisa (La Giaconda)
c. 1503–06
Leonardo da Vinci, 1452–1519
Oil on panel, 38¼ × 21 inches
(97 × 53 cm)

Undoubtedly the jewel in the crown of the Louvre's collection, the *Mona Lisa* must be one of the most familiar paintings in the world. According to Vasari, this picture is a portrait of Mona or Monna (short for Madonna) Lisa, who was born in Florence in 1479 and in 1495 married the Marquis del Giacondo, a Florentine of some standing, hence the painting's other name 'La Giaconda'. This identification though, is still subject to question.

The painting is thought to have been one of those which Leonardo took with him from Florence to Milan in 1506 and then to France in 1516, on the invitation of Francis I. This portrait is believed to be the one which was shown to the Cardinal of Aragon and his secretary in October 1517. It is thought to have been acquired by Francis I from Leonardo himself or from his executor, Francesco Melzi, after his death.

The *Mona Lisa* was stolen from the Salle Carrée in 1911 by Vicenzo Perugia, an Italian workman, thereby increasing its celebrity even further. The painting was found in Florence in 1913 and exhibited in Florence, Rome and Milan before returning to Paris.

Above
Portrait of King Francis I
Clouet, Jean, d.1540
Oil on canvas, 37¾ × 29 inches
(96 × 74 cm)

Ever since this protrait was completed it seems to have been part of the royal collection. Francis I is best described as the epitome of the Renaissance prince: a victorious general, a cultivated man of letters and the arts, the role model for his courtiers and supreme ruler. It was Francis I who successfully enticed Leonardo to France and he who created the nucleus of the collection that would, over time, grow into the national collection held in the Louvre. Originally displayed at Francis' chateau at Fontainebleau, Clouet's painting of the king was transferred to the Louvre in 1848.

Little is known of Jean Clouet's work and this attribution has often been questioned. Père Dan in the seventeenth century attributed this work to 'Jeannet', a pseudonym used by both Jean and his son François, who succeeded him as court painter.

Concert Champêtre c.1510?
Giorgione (Giorgio Barbarelli
[?]), 1477?–1510
Oil on canvas, 43¼ × 54¼ inches
(110 × 138 cm)

Only a handful of paintings can be
attributed to the Venetian painter
Giorgione. His enormous fame rests
on his introduction of a new type of
smallscale painting for private collectors, and his subordination of subject
matter to mood. This particular
painting has a somewhat chequered
history and some historians are
doubtful of Giorgione's authorship.
While some uphold attribution to
Giorgione, others believe it was
painted by the young Titian under
Giorgione's tutelage. The Titianesque
qualities of the painting could be explained by the suggestion that Titian
finished the painting. This is not an
outrageous hypothesis; Giorgione
died very young and left behind
several half-completed canvases,
which were finished by Palma and
Titian. X-rays also appear to support
this, as the position of the female nude
on the right has been altered. Regard-
less of any question of authorship, this
painting of figures in a summer landscape is one of the finest expressions
of Venetian art.

Left
Madonna (La Belle Jardinière)
1507
Raphael (Raffaello Sanzio),
1483–1520
Oil on panel, 48 × 31½ inches
(122 × 80 cm)

During his early career Raphael spent considerable periods in Florence (1504–08) and many of his most celebrated depictions of the Virgin and Child, both with and without landscapes and with and without the figure of the infant St John the Baptist, date from this time. Biographers of Raphael believe that this preoccupation with the theme of the Virgin and Child (or motherhood), in its widest sense, stems from the fact that Raphael's own mother died when he was only eight years old.

The painting was called *La Belle Jardinière* in the early eighteenth century, referring to its country setting. In addition to a number of preparatory drawings, a cartoon for this painting also exists. This picture figures in the inventory drawn up by Le Brun, Keeper of the King's Pictures, in 1683, and because there is no earlier reference to it, it is believed to have been one of the paintings originally acquired by Francis I, whose diplomatic links with Rome and Florence enhanced his collection of contemporary Italian works.

Above
Portrait of Balthasar Castiglione
c.1516
Raphael (Raffaello Sanzio),
1483–1520
Oil on canvas, 32¼ × 26½ inches
(82 × 67 cm)

Summoned to Rome by the Pope in 1508 to work in the Vatican, Raphael also painted many portraits in his later years. Among these were two portraits of Castiglione. Pietro Bembo mentions one in a letter of April 1516 which he describes as nearly finished while, according to a letter to Count Alfonso d'Este from Paulucci of Ferrara in 1519, Castiglione also sat for a second portrait by Raphael.

Castiglione was a diplomat who lived at the courts of several Italian princes including that of Guidobaldo de Montefeltro, whom he considered to be the perfect example of '*il cortegiano*'. In his book of the same name, Castiglione uses the word *cortegiano* not so much to mean a courtier but rather in the sense of a 'man of the court'. In the book, Castiglione defines his ideal of the harmonious life, governed by platonic love and reasoning.

Raphael's portrait reveals a debt to Leonardo. Castiglione is posed in the manner of *Mona Lisa* and Leonardo's painting also inspired a drawing, now in the Cabinet des Dessins in the Louvre.

Above

Madonna with a Rabbit (The Virgin and Child with Saint Catherine) c. 1530
Titian (Tiziano Vecellio), c.1485
Oil on canvas, 27½ × 34 inches
(71 × 87 cm)

Influenced heavily by both Bellini (in the seated figure of the Virgin) and by Giorgione (the landscape), Titian's model for the figure of the Madonna is reputed to have been his wife Cecilia, who died in 1530. The rabbit she holds in her left hand may well be symbolic; when Venus is represented with a rabbit, it symbolizes fecundity (a rabbit figures in Titian's enigmatic allegory of 1516, *Sacred and Profane Love*), but in scenes with the Virgin (such as in Dürer's *Nativity*), the rabbit is often interpreted as a symbol for the Incarnation.

X-ray analysis shows that originally there were several rabbits in the meadow, but these were painted

Above
Portrait of Nicolas Kratzer 1528
Holbein, Hans, 1497-1543
Oil on canvas, 32½ × 26½ inches
(83 × 67 cm)

This three-quarter profile, half-length portrait of Nicolas Kratzer dates from Holbein's first English period. He had worked in Basle as a painter and printer's designer and sought work in England in 1526 when the disturbances of the Reformation led to a decline in patronage. Kratzer, a native of Munich, was King Henry VIII's astronomer and 'deviser of the King's horologes'. Holbein shows Kratzer at his table, holding in his right hand a pair of dividers, in his left a polyhedron with gradated circles engraved on its different faces. On the table are a paper dated 1528, scissors, set-square, a hammer, and a pair of dividers, while on the wall behind him and in a niche are further mathematical instruments.

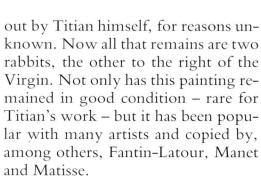

out by Titian himself, for reasons unknown. Now all that remains are two rabbits, the other to the right of the Virgin. Not only has this painting remained in good condition – rare for Titian's work – but it has been popular with many artists and copied by, among others, Fantin-Latour, Manet and Matisse.

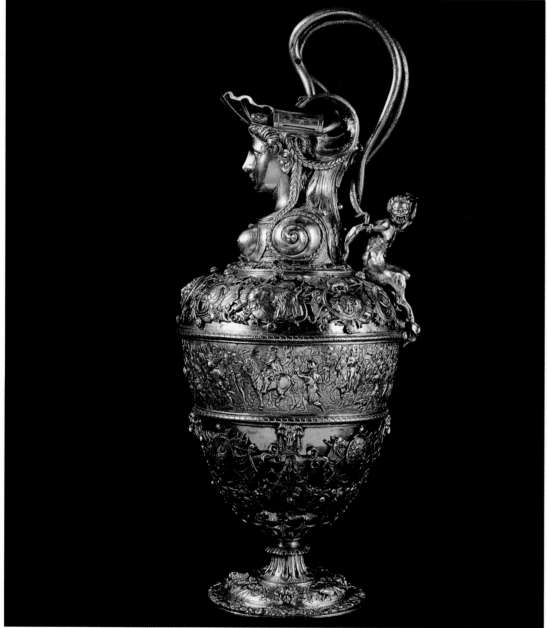

Left
The Pitcher of Charles V,
Flemish, 1558-59
Silver gilt and enamel, 16¾ inches high
(42 cm)

This pitcher, along with its matching
salver, is decorated with scenes commemorating the capture of Tunis in
1535. In 1520 Charles V of Spain had
become Holy Roman Emperor and
France enlisted the help of Ottoman
Turks against him. Tunisia became
the scene of an early East-West power
struggle, with mainly naval confron-
tations between Muslem Turkey and
Christian Spain. In 1534 the youngest
of the Barbarossa brothers, the Cor-
sair Khaireddin, attacked and captured Tunis, Bizerta and La Goulette,
marched inland to take Kairouan and
to join forces with his brother Aruj
who already held the island of Jerba.
Charles V put to sea with 30,000 men;
the bas-relief on the pitcher shows the
embarkation of the imperial troops
after the victory of the Christian
forces at Tunis on July 14 1535.

Left
The Nymph of Fontainebleau
c.1543
Cellini, Benvenuto, 1500–72
Bronze high relief, 80½ × 160 inches
(203 × 409 cm)

Originally intended for the Porte
Dorée at Fontainebleau, this bronze
high relief was made by Cellini
around 1543, during the Florentine
sculptor's second stay in France. The
sculpture was never installed, however. Instead King Henri II gave it as a
gift to his mistress, Diane de Poitiers,
who had the architect Philibert de
l'Orme incorporate it into the trium-
phant portal at Anet in 1562. The
Nymph arrived at the Louvre after the
Revolution and was used by Percier
and Fontaine to decorate the Salon of
the Caryatids.

Right
Caryatid from the Salon of the Caryatids, Louvre
Goujon, Jean, c.1510–1564/1569
Stone, 11 feet 5½ inches high (350 cm)

Jean Goujon was one of the leading
Renaissance artists and introduced to
French sculpture the principles of the
antique. Goujon's caryatids take as
their model the female figures of the
Caryatid Porch on the south of the
Erectheon in Athens. These sculptural elements were favored in the
humanist culture of artistic circles in
Europe and were to be found in illus-
trated editions of the classical author
Vitruvius' writings on architecture.
Rather than supporting the pediment
of a temple, Goujon's caryatids grace
the ballroom of the Louvre Palace.

Above
The Beggars, c.1560
Bruegel, Pieter, c.1525–69
Oil on panel, 7¼ × 8½ inches
(18 × 21.5 cm)

This tiny painting is the only work by
Bruegel in the Louvre. There are
various interpretations of this painting of cripples with a beggar-woman.
Some have seen the fox tails attached
to their cloaks as a reference to the
Gueux, a rebel group formed against
the government in the Netherlands of
the Spanish king Philip II and his chief
counsellor Cardinal Granvella, but
the painting's true meaning is still elu-
sive. The work seems to have satirical
connotations; the cripples wear car-
nival headdresses – a cardboard
crown, a paper helmet, a beret, a cap,
and what looks like a paper bishop's
miter. The painting dates from the
last years of Bruegel's career, when he
displayed a keener interest in nature.
Tiny though it is, Bruegel has still
managed to include a landscape
through the archway in the distance.

Right
The Marriage at Cana (detail),
1562
Veronese (Paolo Caliari), 1528–88
Oil on canvas, 262¼ × 354¼ inches
(666 × 990 cm)

This huge painting, containing 132
figures, was ordered from Veronese
by the Benedictine monks of San
Giorgio, Venice, to decorate their
Palladian refectory. The entire painting was completed in a year and delivered in September 1563, for which
Veronese was paid 324 ducats, a cask
of wine and the cost of his food.
    According to Venetian artistic tra-
dition, the feast here represented is an
ideal banquet in which some of the
great princes of the Renaissance take
part. The newly-wed couple are supposed to be Alfonso Avalos (Charles
V's governor in the Milanais) and
Eleanor of Austria.

Other guests at the table are Francis I and Mary of England (Henry VIII's sister), Suleiman the Magnificent, Vittoria Colonna (Michelangelo's patroness) and Charles V, while the orchestra consists of artists: Veronese himself plays the viola, Tintoretto the violin and Jacopo Bassano the flute. The bearded man who also plays the viola is reputed to be the figure of Palladio, architect of the refectory of San Giorgio as well as of classical villas.

In this large canvas, Veronese abandoned classical one-point perspective in favor of 'multi-focal' perspective, thus retaining the effect of a flat wall surface.

Left
A Saintly King (?), c.1590–1600
El Greco (Domenikos
Theotocopoulos), 1584–1614
Oil on canvas, 46¾ × 37½ inches
(120 × 96 cm)

While most historians agree that El
Greco painted this picture sometime
between 1590 and 1600, there is a great
deal of speculation regarding the
sitter. Because of the fleur-de-lys
emblem on the king's scepter, many
have suggested that the picture is a
portrait of St Louis of France, while
others prefer to read the painting as a
portrait of St Ferdinand of Castile. In
a third version it is not a hagiographic
picture at all, but a historical portrait –
a king of Castile with a connection
with Toledo; perhaps a portrait of
Ferdinand III, or even a Visigothic
king.

To confuse historians further, there
is a replica of this painting in Madrid.
In the Spanish painting the attendant
page is absent, and on the left there is a
view of Toledo under a stormy sky.

Above left
Triton Pendant,
sixteenth century
Gold, enamel and baroque pearl

During the sixteenth century the most
fashionable way to display wealth was
to have clothes strewn with precious
stones and jewelry. Fabulous pieces
shown off against sumptuous silks
and brocades produced a visual splendor which has never been surpassed.

This jeweled pendant takes the
form of a triton, a sort of 'merman'
whose body is made from a mishapen
or 'baroque' pearl and his fish-like tail
of gold. The starting point of this
jewel would have been the pearl, and
the whole pendant is a tribute to the
imagination of the jeweler.

Above right
Star of the Order of Saint-Esprit,
seventeenth century
Diamonds, 4⅓ inches diameter (11 cm)

Bought by the Louvre in 1951, the
diamond Star of the Order of Saint-
Esprit was a gift from Louis XV to
Don Philippe, the Infante of Parma.
This magnificent badge is encrusted
with 400 stones and on the reverse is
inscribed 'LUD.XV.D.D.' indicating
its royal provenance. It is believed to
be the work of a master jeweler called
Jacquemin, one of a number of jewelers who were employed by the court,
since it is characteristic of royal
jewels. In Rigaud's portrait of Philip
V of Spain (1700) the king wears a
similar jeweled badge.

Left
The Clubfooted Boy, 1642
Ribera, José, 1589–1652
Oil on canvas, 64½ × 36¼ inches
(164 × 93 cm)

One of Ribera's last works, this is also one of his most poignant. Spanish artists often painted pictures of beggars, cripples and the poor, an indication of the influence of Caravaggio. Although painted in the tradition of Spanish Realism, Ribera spent most of his lift in Italy, where he was an admirer of the Caravaggesque tradition of painting scenes of 'low life'.

Silhouetted against the landscape, Ribera's crippled youth carries a scrap of paper with the inscription '*Da mihi elemosinam propter amorem Dei*' (give me alms for the love of God). As well as being clubfooted, the youth is also dumb and appeals for charity from passers-by. Yet despite these infirmities, the clubfooted boy carries himself like a proud Spaniard, his crutch over his shoulder like a soldier, and a wide smile fixed on his face.

Right
Portrait of Marianna of Austria, Queen of Spain, 1651
Velásquez, Diego, 1599–1660
Oil on canvas, 82¼ × 49¼ inches
(209 × 125 cm)

The Louvre portrait of the Queen of Spain is one of three paintings of the same sitter; the other two are in the Prado in Madrid and the Kunsthistorisches Museum, Vienna. Marianna was the daughter of Ferdinand III, Emperor of Germany, and of Maria, the sister of Philip IV of Spain. She was born in Vienna in 1634 and was to have married the Infante Balthasar Carlos but he died prematurely. Instead Marianna wed the Infante's widowed uncle in 1649. Since Velasquez was absent from Madrid at the time, the portrait was painted after his return in mid–1651. The Spanish king ordered a copy from Velasquez which was sent to the Escorial Palace. A second copy was eventually sent to Vienna in 1653. Historians now believe that the Prado version is the first painting, done from life, and that the Louvre version is the first copy, originally intended for Vienna, since it is less finished and also smaller than the Prado version.

Left
**Metalwork Grills from the
Galerie d'Apollon,** c.1650
Wrought iron

The wrought iron grills in the Galerie
d'Apollon, which were made in
around 1650 originally for the Château de Maisons, entered the Louvre
collection at the outset of the Revolution. The doors are a magnificent
example of fine iron working: while
the material may be base, the execution belies the heaviness of the
metal in an open, wide and extremely
elegant design. Constructed in 1565
during the reign of Charles IX by the
Queen Mother, Marie de' Medici, the
Galerie d'Apollon was destroyed by
fire in 1661 and subsequently rebuilt
by le Vau with le Brun undertaking
the decoration. Le Brun planned a
painted scheme in honor of Apollo,
symbol of Louis XIV, which was
never completed.

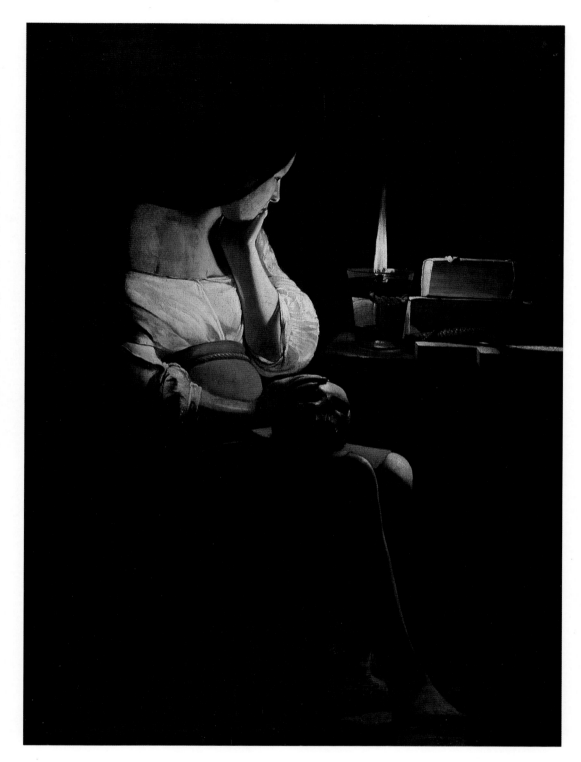

Above
**Saint Mary Magdalen with a
Candle,** 1630–35
La Tour, Georges de, 1593-1652
Oil on canvas, 41½ × 57 inches
(106 × 146 cm)

During the seventeenth century the
figure of Mary Magdalen became the
focus of a cult. A number of written
works attest to the cult of the Magdalen and Provence had two great
sanctuaries dedicated to her: the
grotto of La Sante Baume and the
Saintes Maries de la Mer.

Mary Magdalen was seen as the
perfect lover of Christ, beautiful, fal-
lible, yet repentant. It is possible that
La Tour was inspired by Italian or
Dutch artists; the saint's body is hid-
den in darkness, her face illuminated
by a candle. On the table are some
books and resting on a wooden cross
is a blood-stained scourge, a reminder
of the violence of Mary Magdalen's
penitence.

The Inspiration of the Poet,
c.1636–38
Poussin, Nicolas, 1594–1665
Oil on canvas, 51½ inches × 83½ inches
(132 cm × 213 cm)

The warm coloring of this painting reveals the Titianesque influence in Poussin's work. This work was painted at the end of Poussin's first period in Rome, sometime around 1636–38 and was acquired by the Louvre in 1911.

Apollo, accompanied by winged *putti* and the muse of Poetry, is about to crown a poet who writes under the influence of divine inspiration. To what the painting exactly alludes is unknown. There are, however, other works related to this painting, including *The Inspiration of Anacreon* (Dulwich Picture Gallery and a version in Hanover) and *Parnassus* (Prado), as well as the frontispiece to an edition of Virgil published by the Imprimerie Royale in 1641–42. The model for the muse, also recognizable in other works from this period by Poussin, may have been Anna Dughet, whom he married in 1630.

Village Fête, 1639
Claude le Lorrain (Claude
Gellée), 1600–82
Oil on canvas, 40½ inches × 53¼ inches
(103 cm × 135 cm)

This painting, along with its companion piece *A Sea-Port*, was given to
Louis XIV in 1693 by the royal architect and gardener le Nôtre. *Village
Fête* was painted fairly early on in
Claude's career and was influenced by
Flemish painting. At the center of the
composition is a group of trees, while
on either side are openings through
which light appears. This arrange-
ment had been used by Flemish landscape artists from the time of Breugel
and Claude continued this tradition in
Rome, where he spent most of his life.
Through the opening on the right is a
city bathed in golden light, a touch
that is more reminiscent of the Roman
Campagna than of the North. Following the usual practice in the Low
Countries, Claude often employed
other artists to paint in the small
figures in his landscapes.

Left
The Joys of the Regency, 1622-23
Rubens, Sir Peter Paul, 1577-1640
Oil on canvas, 155 × 116¼ inches
(394 × 295 cm)

In 1620 the Queen Mother, Marie de' Medici, became reconciled with her son, Louis XIII, at Brissac and turned her attention to her Paris home, the Palais Luxembourg, and its decoration. Rubens was summoned by the Queen in 1621 to carry out decorations for two galleries, one in her honor and one in honor of Henri IV. She decided to begin work on her own gallery, and Rubens was asked to submit sketches for the design. By June 1623, Rubens had delivered the first nine paintings in the scheme and was planning to put the finishing touches to them in Paris. The Galerie Medici was inaugurated on the occasion of the marriage of Henrietta Maria of France and the English King, Charles I, which had taken place on May 8. *The Joys of the Regency*, however, was hastily painted in Paris in order to replace the painting of *Marie de Medicis Leaving Paris*, evidently a subject which did not please the queen. The projected gallery in honor of Henri IV was never carried out, because of Marie's subsequent fall from favor, and only sketches of it survive, along with two unfinished paintings now in the Uffizi Gallery, Florence.

Above
The Gypsy Woman, c.1630
Hals, Frans, 1580-1666
Oil on panel, 22¾ × 20½ inches
(58 × 52 cm)

This type of painting – a portrait of an 'ordinary' person - was practiced in Rome by the followers of Caravaggio and brought to Holland by Gerrit van Honthorst (1590-1656). This is one of the most famous examples of Hals' 'genre' style, but in the context of Dutch painting of the seventeenth century pictures of this type are comparatively rare, since most genre subjects contained more than one figure. Although most probably painted from life, this painting cannot really be considered a portrait in the strict sense, since it would not have been commissioned by or intended for the model. It is painted naturalistically and on a small scale; it is easy to see Hals' direct method of laying paint and his ability to suggest details by loose brush strokes. Although it dates from around the same time as *Hille Bobbe*, the *Mulatto* and the *Jolly Drinker*, the smile on the gypsy woman's face is unlike the wild laughter of some of Hals' other genre portraits.

Bathsheba Bathing, 1654
Rembrandt Van Rijn, 1606–69
Oil on canvas, 56 × 56 inches
(142 × 142 cm)

This painting comes from a troubled period in Rembrandt's life. In the year that it was painted, the model for the figure of Bathsheba, Hendrickje Stoffels, was summoned before a church hearing and banished from the church, having been found guilty of being Rembrandt's mistress. The painting of *Bathsheba Bathing* no doubt contributed to her being ostracized from the religious community. A young peasant girl from Randorp, Hendrickje was 22 years old when Rembrandt engaged her as a servant in 1649. In the same year his son Titus' nurse, Geertghe Dircx, who had also been his mistress and with whom he was having a legal dispute, had to be removed to a lunatic asylum. Despite her troubles, Hendrickje remained Rembrandt's faithful companion until her death in around 1662.

Rembrandt's painting of *Bathsheba Bathing* (along with *Danae*, for which his wife Saskia van Uylenburch had been the model) is one of only two nude portraits in which Rembrandt was concerned with depicting the sensuality of woman. Bathsheba is shown not as an impersonal, idealized beauty or goddess, but as a real flesh-and-blood woman. X-ray analysis shows that at first Rembrandt intended the head of Bathsheba to be more upright and the thighs to be draped with a piece of fabric, which he subsequently removed.

The Lacemaker, c.1664
Vermeer, Jan, 1632–75 (known as
Jan Vermeer of Delft)
Oil on canvas, 9½ × 8¼ inches
(24 × 21 cm)

Now considered to be one of the greatest painters of all time, Vermeer's reputation is in fact only just over a century old. On March 16, 1696 an anonymous sale in Amsterdam featured this painting among no less than 21 of Vermeer's pictures. His only known patron during his lifetime was a local baker in Delft, and after Vermeer's death a Delft bookseller, Jacob Dissius, is said to have owned around 20 of his works, but it is not known whether he acquired them directly from the artist; they represented over half Vermeer's total output.

This picture belongs to a group of small, almost square paintings in which a single figure is shown half-length. Recent lightening of the varnish has also restored much of the density of the colors to the work. Renoir declared that this painting was the most beautiful in the world. Salvador Dali, commissioned by an American amateur to make a copy, produced his own Surrealist version of the painting, while André Malraux believed that the model for *The Lacemaker* and Vermeer's other works was Catherine Vermeer, the artist's wife.

CHAPTER FOUR

Classicism, Romanticism and Realism

Although separated by only 16 years, Hyacinthe Rigaud's portrait of *Louis XIV* (1701) and Jean Antoine Watteau's *The Embarkation for the Island of Cythera* (1717) reflect two very different moods. The former is characterized by its solemnity and ostentation; it is academic and greatly influenced by the taste of the court. The latter painting is noteworthy for its refined and dreamy elegance.

Following the death of Louis XIV (1717), many of the nobility chose not to return to their ancestral homes in the provinces but to remain in Paris, where they built for themselves elegant town houses called hotels. Often erected on narrow or irregular sites, these hotels

offered little opportunity for grand imposing facades. Instead, the designers turned their attention to the interiors, where they introduced the more intimate, smallscale and airy Rococo style. With Louis's death, the power of the 'absolute monarchy' declined and with it state-sponsored art patronage. Increasingly, artists became dependent on private patrons.

By 1700 Charles Lebrun's influence as supervisor of the King's artistic projects and as director of the Royal Academy of Painting and Sculpture had begun to wane. Lebrun had established for the Academy a rigid curriculum and a system of tabulating the merits of artists, past and present, into categories such as drawing, expression and proportion. Under this system, the artists of classical antiquity received the highest praise and marks, followed by Raphael and Poussin, but Venetian painters, who emphasized color over drawing, ranked low, while the Dutch and Flemish artists were ranked lower still. Subject matter was similarly ranked, with history paintings – either classical or Biblical stories – at the top and still lifes at the bottom.

Despite these rigid rules, a counter-movement in painting began to emerge and by 1700 the members of the Academy were split into two camps over the issue of drawing versus color. The conservatives or 'Poussinistes' defended Poussin's view that drawing appealed to the mind and was superior to color. The 'Rubenistes,' on the other hand, believed that color was truer to nature than drawing, since drawing was based on reason which appealed only to the select and expert viewer, while color appealed to everyone. While the argument may seem pointless to us today, this debate had revolutionary implications at the time, as the Rubenistes were implying that ordinary people could also be the judges of artistic values, whereas the Renaissance view of art was that it could only be appreciated by a suitably educated elite.

In 1717 the Rubenistes triumphed when Jean Antoine Watteau was admitted to the Academy on the basis of his submission painting *The Embarkation for the Island of Cythera*, a picture that violated all of Lebrun's academic rules of painting. Furthermore, Watteau's painting did not conform to any established 'genre' or category of painting: it did not contain a noble or elevating theme but was a scene of elegant and refined society in a mythological setting. The Academy accommodated Watteau's painting in a newly developed genre, the *fêtes galantes* (elegant fêtes or entertainments).

Watteau's painting is actually entitled *The Pilgrimage to Cythera* and the alternative title under which it has become famous is in fact incorrect, since the pilgrims are already on the island of Venus and are preparing to depart, having made their offerings of garlands at the statue of the goddess. The subject was inspired by

Left Watteau: *Jupiter and Antiope.* One of the great figures of Rococo art, Watteau's work violated the academic rules of painting but was still accepted by the Academy.

Above Fragonard: *The Music Lesson*. Like Watteau, Fragonard's painting was accommodated by the Academy despite its lighthearted non-classical mood.

Rubens' *Garden of Love* but Watteau's handling of the subject, with its curving composition, clear colors and overall mood of happiness tinged with nostalgia, was to be extremely influential on French painting in the eighteenth century.

The work of Watteau symbolizes a major shift in both French art and society. Most subsequent French Rococo painting follows the Rubeniste style – small in scale and perfect for decorating the interiors of the new hotels, with its sensual handling and subject matter. Meanwhile most of the decorative works commissioned by Louis XIV continued to adorn, or were returned to, the various palaces for which they were executed. Rigaud's portrait of the king, symbol of the French monarchy, had in fact been intended as a gift for Louis' grandson, Philip V of Spain, but when he saw

the painting Louis liked it so much that he kept it, and had a copy made and sent to Spain. Watteau died at the early age of 37 but he nevertheless had a great many followers, the finest of whom was undoubtedly Honoré Fragonard.

Fragonard was accepted by the Academy as a 'history painter' due to the fact that his academy submission work was *The High Priest Chaereas Sacrificing Himself for Callirrhoe* (1765), a cartoon for a tapestry designed for the Gobelin factory but never executed. Fragonard soon abandoned this type of subject matter, however, and devoted himself to the pleasant and occasionally frivolous paintings for which he is most famous. An even franker Rubeniste than Watteau, Fragonard's brushwork is reminiscent of Rubens' oil sketches. Unlike Watteau, Fragonard lived long past his own era; he died forgotten and in poverty after the French Revolution.

The Rubenistes cleared the way for a new interest in the work of the Dutch masters. While the works of Jean-Baptiste Siméon Chardin may, with some reservations, be termed Rococo, he was nevertheless the finest painter of still lifes and genre scenes in the Dutch style. In many respects Chardin's still lifes are akin to his genre scenes, in that they depict similarly modest environments. The objects in the still lifes could be found in any kitchen in France, while at the same time they are also the symbols of the 'common man.'

The Rubenistes remained pre-eminent until the Revolution. During the heyday of Napoleon Bonaparte, however, they suffered a reversal of fortunes and the classicizing doctrines of the Poussinistes once more became the official academic style in art, exemplified above all in the work of David.

Despite the strength of French painting, it seems strange that during the eighteenth century those responsible for the royal collection should have acquired so few works by contemporary Italian artists. The Venetian painters Sebastiano Ricci and Giovanni Pellegrini, who caused a sensation with their visits to Paris in the first quarter of the century, are represented only by their 'election' pieces to the Académie Royale, which entered the Louvre during the Revolution, while a painting sent to Louis XV had already been lost.

One Venetian masterpiece which became part of the Louvre collection during the Revolution was the series of twelve *Venetian Festivals* by Francesco Guardi, recounting the various episodes in the election of the Doge of Venice, Alviso Mocenigo, in 1763. In this series, Guardi had been influenced by engravings made after that other master of the Venetian *veduta* (view), Antonio Canaletto, and he produced a picturesque record of Venetian ceremonies and festivals.

Louis XV was not a keen collector, but contemporary sovereigns in the rest of Europe were busy buying contemporary art: Frederick III of Prussia acquired works by Watteau, Lancret and Chardin; his sister Louise-Ullrich of Sweden, on the advice of the French Ambassador Tessin, bought Boucher and Chardin, while Catherine the Great, Empress of Russia, bought an entire collection belonging to the Baron de Thiers after his death in 1770, which contained both historical and major contemporary works. Louis XV, on the other hand, did not own a single Watteau or Fragonard, but he did commission a number of *sopraportes* (paintings designed to be placed over doorways) from Chardin and Lancret for his various châteaux. Many works by Boucher and Fragonard purchased during his reign were not paintings but cartoons for tapestries. Louis XVI appears to have been only a little more inclined to contemporary art than his predecessor, and most of the eighteenth-century art which entered the Louvre did so through confiscation during the revolutions or as a result of donations and purchases in the nineteenth century.

Work that was considered frivolous and of little interest during Louis XV's reign had to wait until the mid-nineteenth century before there was a revival of interest. By this time Chardin was particularly sought after and seven of his paintings were bought before the Second Empire. But the most outstanding work of the eighteenth century, constituting the major part of the Louvre's collection from this period, was acquired through the bequest of the La Caze collection in 1869. Dr Louis La Caze, himself a painter, was also a keen collector. In addition to numerous other works, La Caze donated no less than eight works by Watteau (including the *Judgment of Paris* and *Gilles*), which had previously been in the collection of Vivant Denon, Directeur of the Musée Napoléon.

Spanish painting in the Louvre was also under-represented until the nineteenth century, when Spain and Spanish art became fashionable and many new collections were formed. The earliest of the Spanish works in the Louvre were brought to France by French generals under Joseph Bonaparte, returning from the Peninsular War. The most prodigious collection of Spanish art was that of Louis Philippe, assembled for him by Baron Taylor, which contained hundreds of works by the Spanish masters, especially Goya and Zurbarán. Although exhibited at the Louvre from 1838–1848, the Spanish collection was returned to the Orléans family after the 1848 Revolution, and was subsequently broken up and sold in 1853. The earlier collection of Spanish art sent to the Musée Napoléon in 1813 had been returned to Spain by 1815 following Napoleon's downfall. Once again, the Louvre had to await the later nineteenth-century purchases and the generosity of La Caze before its Spanish collection was back to strength.

The third quarter of the eighteenth century saw a gradual turning of the tide in European art. While artists such as Fragonard and Tiepolo continued to create works in the Rococo manner, others, in the name of 'Reason' and 'Nature,' were reacting against the remnants of baroque artificiality. The two concepts of Reason and Nature had been proclaimed as the ultimate values by the thinkers of the Enlightenment. Writers such as Hume, Diderot, Voltaire and Rousseau maintained that human life should be governed by Reason and the common good rather than by tradition or any established authority. In art the advancement of the concept of reason signified a return to the doctrines of the Poussinistes. The return to reason, to nature and to a new morality in art meant a return to the ancients, to what the German critic and archeologist Winckelmann called the 'noble simplicity' and 'calm grandeur' of the Greeks.

While it is generally accepted that Rome was the birthplace of this new 'Neoclassical' style, most of its early protagonists were not Italians but northern visitors. It was in Rome that Jacques-Louis David, a young French painter trained in the Rococo tradition, executed *The Oath of the Horatii* (1784), which stunned public and artists alike when it was exhibited at the Paris Salon of 1785. Its sober realism, simplification of form and the overall heroic and classical tone of the subject matter were to be an important influence on painting in the future.

During Louis XIV's reign the policy of encouraging

the painting of historical subjects maintained by the Directeur des Bâtiments, the Comte d'Angivillier, meant that the king commissioned and purchased large paintings, often of Greek or Roman subjects, which were used as templates for tapestries. During the Revolution, the government purchased a number of additional works that had been commissioned during the monarchy, while others were confiscated from the nobility. During the Empire, huge paintings of contemporary history were commissioned to glorify the Napoleonic era.

While David was an ardent admirer of Napoleon and executed several large works glorifying the Emperor, including *The Consecration of the Emperor Napoleon and the Coronation of the Empress Josephine* (1805-7), and *Napoleon in his Study* (1807), he was eclipsed by his own pupil, Jean-Antoine Gros, as the foremost painter of the Napoleonic myth. In works by Gros such as his portrait *Napoleon at Arcole* (1796), painted in Milan soon after a series of victories gave France control of the Lombard Plain, and *Napoleon Visiting the Plague House at Jaffa* (1798), the first important signs appear of the Romantic sensibility that was to pervade nineteenth-century European art. Much as Gros respected the doctrines of both David and the Poussinistes, he was impelled toward the color and drama of Rubens and the Baroque.

After Napoleon's downfall, David spent his last years in exile in Belgium and the mantle of Neoclassicism fell on his other pupil, Jean-Auguste-Dominique Ingres. A supporter of Bonaparte, Ingres went to Rome in 1806 and remained there for 18 years. It was only after his return to Paris in 1824 that he became the leading exponent of the Davidian tradition.

The Neoclassical style that only half a century earlier had seemed revolutionary was now set into a rigid dogma backed by conservative opinion and endorsed by the state. But Ingres' work is much less doctrinaire than his theories. While he held that drawing was superior to painting, his smooth figures of odalisques are not simply embodiments of classical ideals of beauty and are, furthermore, set off by the rich tones and textures of the interiors which they inhabit. For Ingres, history painting as defined by Poussin and David remained a lifelong ambition, but one with which he constantly struggled. It was in portraiture, which he claimed to dislike, that he achieved his clearest mastery.

Thus the Enlightenment not only liberated reason, but paradoxically also helped to create the new wave of emotionalism known as Romanticism. While the Poussinistes and rationalists saw nature as the ultimate source of reason, the Romantics saw nature as ever-changing, sublime and picturesque, and in the name of nature they worshipped freedom, power, love, the Greeks, the Middle Ages, indeed anything that aroused a response; they even worshipped emotion itself. Extremists among the Romantics believed that the Romantic attitude could be expressed only through direct action and not through works of art, because art

requires discipline and detachment; yet in order to make experiences and emotions concrete, artists required a style. Since the Romantic artist was in revolt against the old order, his style could not be the established style of the time. As Romantic artists searched

for past phases in history with which they felt a link, they inspired multiple revivals of neglected styles. Painters such as Théodore Géricault and Eugène Delacroix rebelled against the meticulous draftsmanship and detail of Poussin, David and Ingres to use more

Above Chardin: *Still Life with Pipe and Drinking Glasses*, typical of the naturalistic tendency that persisted throughout the eighteenth century alongside Rococo.
Overleaf David's neoclassical work *The Intervention of the Sabine Women*.

vivid color and broader, more open brushwork in the manner of Rubens, Hals, Velásquez and Goya.

During the reigns of Louis XVIII and Charles X the Louvre collection acquired several masterpieces by living artists which were purchased directly from the Salon. The royal administration bought Delacroix's *The Barque of Dante and Virgil* (1822) and *The Massacre at Chios* (1824). Normally works of art were chosen to accord with conventional taste but these purchases show that the administration could, on occasion, be quite daring. In 1825 the museum bought Géricault's *The Raft of the Medusa*, the subject of which was a contemporary not a historical event, and one of extreme political delicacy, a fact that was exploited by the opposition to attack the existing regime.

Purchases of Delacroix's works continued at the Salon and his masterpiece *Liberty Leading the People* was bought by Louis Philippe in 1831. But the government feared the influence of the painting's subject and allowed it to be exhibited only for a few weeks in the Musée du Luxembourg before returning it to Delacroix's studio for 'safe-keeping.' Exhibited only three times in 1849, 1855 and 1861, *Liberty Leading the People* finally found its home in the Louvre in 1874, more than 40 years after it was purchased.

The Romantics, with their worship of nature, raised nature itself to a new significance and it was landscape painting that conveyed many of the most profoundly experienced emotions. Until the early eighteenth century, painting had been confined to the artist's studio. Watercolor and oil sketches could be taken direct from nature, but to paint a complete picture outside was considered technically and aesthetically undesirable. The equipment required for painting was rather cumbersome, and the process of oil painting itself was considered too slow to capture on canvas the constantly changing effects of light on a scene being directly observed. The Romantics, however, upset this centuries-old outlook and tradition. While many painters continued to work in their studios others, such as Camille Corot, began to paint *en plein air*, making use of the newly devised products of the Industrial Revolution – ready-prepared oil paints in tubes, new portable easels and artist's stools. The pictures painted 'on the spot' tended to be small and lacking in the precise details of earlier landscape work.

Sadly, the achievements of many of the greatest Romantic landscape artists, in particular Caspar David Friedrich, John Constable and Joseph Turner, are under-represented in the Louvre. Constable's *View in the Park at Helmingham* (1800) and *View of Salisbury* (1800) were only acquired by the Louvre in 1948 and 1952 respectively, and Turner is represented only by a single, late work, *Landscape with a River and a Bay in the Background* (c.1835-40) which was bought by the Louvre in 1967.

Not only did the Industrial Revolution dramatically alter the materials of painting, but the changes wrought by it on society by the mid-nineteenth century were reflected by artists in the themes they chose. Honoré Daumier is best known for his satirical cartoons and received little acclaim in his lifetime for his paintings depicting the contemporary human condition. While many of his works have contemporary themes, Daumier's style is akin to that of the great Romantic, Delacroix. Other mid-nineteenth-century painters, however, were to react against Romanticism not only in their subject matter but by adopting a radically different style. As early as 1846, the poet and critic Charles Baudelaire called for a painting that would reflect what he called the 'heroism of modern life', a call that was transformed into an artistic creed by Gustave Courbet.

Courbet believed that the Romantic stress on emotions and imagination was an escape from the realities of the time, and maintained that the artist must rely on direct experience, must be a 'Realist.' Courbet could not, as his famous statement tells us, 'paint an angel because I have never seen one.' Courbet's work, along with that of his contemporary Jean-François Millet, was condemned at the time for its 'vulgarity' and for its apparent lack of spiritual content. For the Realists, the subject matter was of primary importance and style only a means to an end. Conservative outrage at the time is understandable, since the Realists rejected official academic teaching and condemned all traditional subjects, whether drawn from religion, mythology, allegory or history. Consequently it is hardly surprising that the works of the Realists were not acquired by the Louvre until the end of the century, after the artists' deaths. Many of Courbet's works were purchased by the Louvre from the sale of his studio in 1881, the same year that Juliette Courbet presented *The Burial at Ornans* (1850) to the museum. Likewise several works by Millet were acquired only at the posthumous sale of his work in 1875.

More surprising than the official art world's neglect of the Realists is the poor treatment that the Louvre afforded that most ardent Classicist and follower of Raphael, Ingres, despite contemporary acclaim for his paintings. Once again, it was only after Ingres' death that several of his works entered the collection, by means of bequests (notably by the Rivière family in 1870) and by purchases in the late nineteenth century.

Left Géricault: *Mounted Officer of the Imperial Guard.* Géricault was one of the most significant and original painters of the French Romantic movement.

Left
Portrait of Louis XIV, King of France, 1701-2
Rigaud, Hyacinthe, 1659-1743
Oil on canvas, 108¼ × 75¾ inches
(277 × 194 cm)

This official portrait was commissioned by Louis XIV and was originally intended to be sent to the Spanish court as a royal gift. Louis, however, was so impressed with the painting, which portrayed him with all the trappings of monarchical power – including the ancient and famous so-called Sword of Charlemagne at his side – that he decided to keep it at Versailles and have a copy sent to Madrid.

It is likely that only the face of the king was painted from life, with the body 'superimposed' and painted from a stand-in model. The whole canvas was later inlaid in a larger one and was finished in Rigaud's studio with the help of Sevin de la Pennaye, who usually assisted Rigaud with the elaboration of costumes and accessories. The painting is signed 'Hyacinthe Rigaud et Sevin'.

Above
The Elector of Bavaria's Writing Bureau, c.1715
Boulle, André Charles, 1642-1732
Ebony, with mother of pearl, marquetry and leather,
78¾ inches × 63 inches (200 × 160 cm)

Boulle, created Ebéniste du Roi in 1672, was one of those rare craftsmen who are completely at ease working in a variety of fields. In addition to the arms of the Elector inscribed on the central panel of this magnificent desk, the clock also bears his coat of arms.

Left
Gilles, c.1719
Watteau, Jean-Antoine, 1684–1721
Oil on canvas, 72½ × 58¾ inches
(184 × 149 cm)

According to tradition, this painting
was used by a dealer called Meunier as
a sign in the window of his shop in the
Cour du Carousel. Actually written
on the canvas, albeit in chalk, was the
inscription:
*Que Pierrot serait content
S'il avait l'art de vous plaire.*
(Pierrot will be happy if he can please
you) almost begging someone to buy
the painting! The large scale and direct
presentation of the principal character
of Gilles are exceptional in Watteau's
work and have led many to believe
that the painting's original function
was as a theatrical signboard. In fact a
play, *Danae*, was premiered in 1721, a
week after Watteau's death, in which
Harlequin was changed into a donkey. There is indeed a donkey in Watteau's painting, and attempts have
been made to identify the different
Italian comedy actors.

Above
The Ray, 1728
Chardin, Jean-Baptiste-Siméon,
1699–1779
Oil on canvas, 45 × 57½ inches
(114 × 146 cm)

The Ray, along with *The Buffet*, was
Chardin's 'diploma' painting for his
entry into the Académie Royale de
Peinture et de Sculpture in 1728. Contrary to the usual practice, Chardin
was accepted and admitted on the
same day. Furthermore, the Académie did not ask him to submit a new
work painted specially for the occasion, as was usually the case, but
accepted *The Ray* and *The Buffet* as
diploma works.
    Chardin's still lifes were often mis-
taken, even in his own lifetime, for
Flemish works. The source of inspiration for *The Ray*, particularly in the
treatment of the cat, is the work of the
Flemish painter Jan Fyt (1611-61).
Chardin's work was later itself to provide inspiration to a number of artists:
Cézanne made a drawing of this
painting, and Matisse copied it.

Previous pages 132-33
**The Embarkation for the Island
of Cythera**, 1717
Watteau, Jean-Antoine, 1684–1721
Oil on canvas, 50½ × 76 inches
(129 × 194 cm)

In 1712 Watteau's nomination for
membership of the Academy was
accepted, but he was only finally
formally received into the Academy
in 1717, with the presentation of a
painting then entitled *Pilgrimage to
Cythera*. This had been a traditional
theme in French poetry ever since the
Middle Ages, with love depicted as a
voyage to a beautiful and blessed
island. At the beginning of the
eighteenth century, the idea of the
departure for Cythera recurs in
numerous ballets and operas. Now
better known by its erroneous title,
Watteau's painting actually depicts a
group of pilgrims leaving the en-
chanted island, having placed their
flower tributes at the statue of Venus.
The subject is taken from Rubens' *Jardin d'Amour* in the Galerie Medici and
the atmosphere is Italian.

Above
Diana Bathing, 1742
Boucher, François, 1703–70
Oil on canvas, 22½ × 28¾ inches
(56 × 73 cm)

This work, painted for the Salon of 1742, is undoubtedly Boucher's masterpiece. Here the goddess of the hunt, Diana, is portrayed with a female attendant, after bathing in a stream while following her hunt. Beside her are the spoils of the day's hunt, a hare and several birds, while at her feet rests her quiver and arrows. One of Diana's hunting dogs drinks from the stream and the other looks into the reeds. Perhaps Acteon is hiding in the undergrowth, so far unseen by the goddess, who for spying on her will transform him into a deer and

have him killed by his own hunting dogs. Unaware of Acteon, Diana and her attendant are oblivious also of the spectator's gaze.

After his first royal commission in 1735, Boucher became the leading decorator of royal palaces and private residences, and was especially favored by royal mistress Madame de Pompadour. In 1765 Boucher was made Premier Peintre du Roi, but by then his reputation was in decline, and he was often seen simply as a painter of decorative works. More recent artists, including Renoir, another great painter of nudes bathing, have praised Boucher's understanding of the female body. Renoir said that *Diana Bathing* was the first painting that 'captivated' him and one that he admired all his life.

Above right
Women Bathing, c.1755–56
Fragonard, Jean-Honoré, 1732–1806
Oil on canvas, 25¼ × 31½ inches
(64 × 80 cm)

This early work, bequeathed to the Louvre by Dr La Caze in 1869, was probably painted before Fragonard made his first visit to Italy in 1756. He was almost certainly inspired by Rubens' depiction of the Nereids in *The Arrival of the Queen*, from the series of paintings celebrating the life of Marie de Medici in the Galerie Medicis.

Fragonard achieved a luminous transparency using a skilful combination of scumbling (applying paper to wet paint in order to remove any excess), glazes and impasto (pure pigment) in the highlights. The color is well preserved, aided by painting '*alla prima*' (without interruption); the lack of subsequent reworking or repainting has left the pigments as bright as they were when first applied.

Right
The Spring 1756
Sèvres porcelain and bronze gilt,
13 × 16¾ inches (33 × 43 cm)

This Sèvres porcelain piece is typical
of a type of work much sought after in
the eighteenth century. It appears that
this piece was sold by the Sèvres
manufacturers in 1757 to a dealer,
Lazare Duvaux, who immediately re-
sold it to a second dealer, a Monsieur
Herbert. It eventually entered the
Louvre along with other pieces in the
magnificent Thiers collection.

This was the last Sèvres piece to be
mounted in bronze. The source of the
spring is personified by the figure of a
young girl, who sits atop a miniature
hill and is overturning her water jar to
irrigate the land and water a gilt
bronze tree to her left.

The Departure of the Doge in the 'Bucentaur' for the Ascension Day Ceremony, c.1764
Guardi, Francesco, 1712-93
Oil on canvas, 26¼ × 39½ inches
(67 × 101 cm)

This painting is one of a series of 12 pictures commemorating the festivities at the coronation of the Venetian Doge, Alviso IV Mocenigo, in 1763. For this series, Guardi copied the scenes drawn by that other famous Venetian painter of *vedute* (views), Canaletto, which had been engraved by Giambattist Brustolon.

Under the Empire, the series was broken up: seven remained in the Louvre; the cities of Toulouse, Grenoble and Brussels were each sent one; and two were sent to Nantes. The Toulouse scene was later returned to the Louvre through an exchange of paintings.

Two of the paintings represent the feast of the Bucentaur, the most extravagant of all the Venetian festivals. This took place each year on Ascension Day, the anniversary of the setting out of the expedition led by Doge Pietro Orsini in c. 1000 AD to conquer Dalmatia. In the magnificent state barge, the *Bucentaur*, the Doge visited the Lido and celebrated the marriage of the 'Pearl of the Adriatic' to the sea by casting a gold ring into the lagoon. This canvas shows the *Bucentaur* leaving Venice, while another in the Louvre depicts the Doge hearing Mass at San Niccolo del Lido.

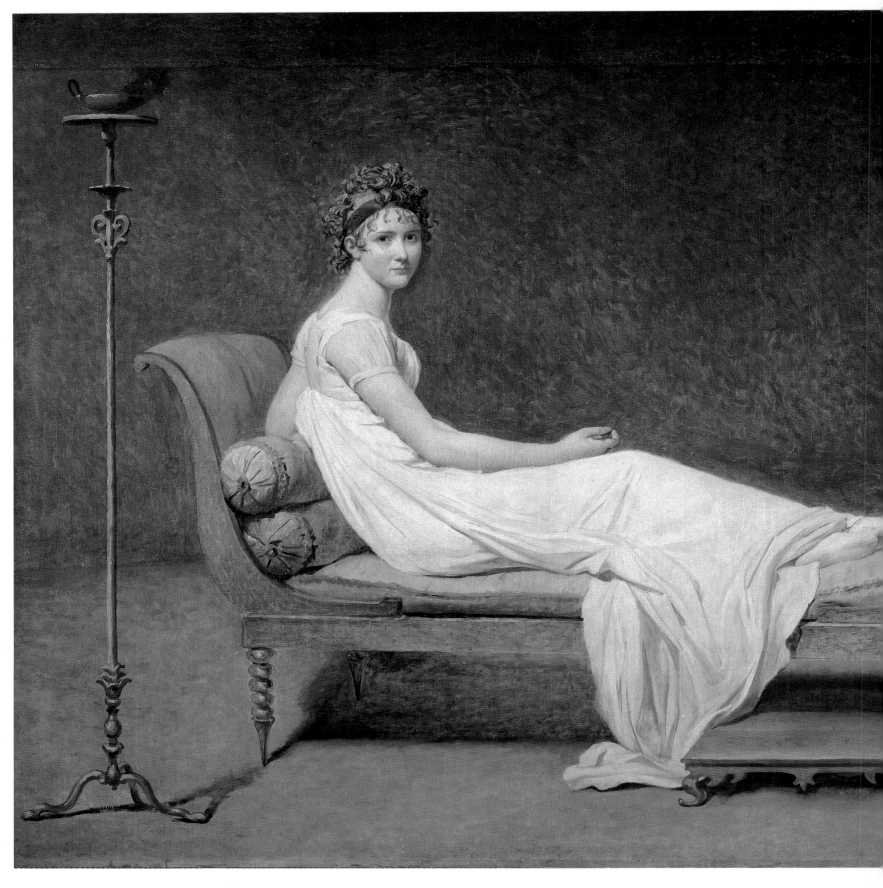

Above
Madame Récamier, 1800
David, Jacques Louis, 1748-1825
Oil on canvas, 68 × 95¼ inches
(174 × 244 cm)

In 1800 Madame Récamier commissioned David to paint her portrait, but she proved to be an unreliable model. Furthermore, tension between David and his subject was increased when he discovered that the painter Gérard had also been commissioned to paint her.

'*La belle Juliette*', as she was known, was then 23 years old and at the beginning of her career as a reigning beauty. Married to a banker much older than herself, she was all her life to arouse passionate feelings in her male suitors: her last conquest was the poet Chateaubriand. Here David shows the languid beauty in a relaxed pose reclining on an 'antique' sofa. The furnishings all point to the fashion for classical antiquity which was to reach its height under the

Empire. The effect is further enhanced by Juliette's simple tunic with its loosely flowing folds, which reveal her bare feet. According to legend, the accessories were painted by David's pupil Ingres and, following his usual method, having sketched in the pose, David concentrated on the head, which is nearly finished and contrasts strongly with the unfinished background.

Above

The Countess del Carpio,
c.1791-92

Goya y Lucientes, Francisco José
de, 1746-1828

Oil on canvas, 71¼ × 48 inches
(181 × 122 cm)

This picture, which only entered the
Louvre in 1953, is considered to be
one of Goya's finest female portraits.
Maria Rita Barrenechea y Morante,
born around 1750, married the Count
del Carpio in November 1775. The
Countess died in 1795 and many
critics have seen her expression as a
depiction of anxiety at the approach of
death. Others, however, attribute the
mood of the painting to Goya's own
mysterious and traumatic illness in
1792, which left him totally deaf. The
picture in fact dates from what is
called Goya's 'gray period', just before his illness. We do know that the
Countess was a cultivated woman, a
poet, whose work was published in
1783. The simplicity of the portrait –
the plain background and lack of
rhetorical devices – add to the
mysterious quality of the painting.

**The Consecration of the Emperor
Napoleon I and the Coronation of
the Empress Josephine**, 1805–07
David, Jacques Louis, 1748–1825
Oil on canvas, 242½ × 382½ inches
(621 × 979 cm)

David was commissioned by
Napoleon to paint this large composition to commemorate his consecration, which had taken place in Notre
Dame in Paris in December 1804.
While the general composition is
derived from Rubens' *Coronation of
Queen Marie de Medici*, David's usual
method of working was to produce
numerous studies, both painted and
drawn. The best known study is the
Portrait of Pope Pius VII, also in the
Louvre. In addition, David constructed a scale model, in which he
arranged costumed dolls in order to
organize the placement of the figures.

David originally intended to portray the event accurately and to show
Napoleon crowning himself. The
Emperor had placed the crown on his
own head and thereby avoided giving
a pledge of obedience by the temporal
power to the Pope. Napoleon, however, did not want to immortalize this
somewhat disrespectful action on
canvas, so he had David paint the
coronation of Josephine, with the
Pope blessing the Empress. At first
David depicted the Pope with his
hands resting on his knees, but
Napoleon is reputed to have re-
marked 'I did not bring him all this
way to do nothing!'

Arranged around the altar of Notre
Dame, near Napoleon, are the chief
dignitaries: Cambacères (the Lord
Chancellor), Marshal Berthier (Grand
Veneur) Talleyrand (the Lord
Chamberlain) and Lebrun (the Chief
Treasurer). Carrying the Empress'
train is Madame de la Rochefoucault,
while behind are Napoleon's sisters
and his brothers Louis and Joseph. In
front of the central stand are some of
those whom Napoleon created marshal, while in it is Marie Laetitia,
Madame Mère (Napoleon's mother),
who in fact was not present at the
ceremony but at home in Corsica.

Bonaparte Visiting the Plague House at Jaffa, c.1800
Gros, Jean-Antoine, 1771–1835
Oil on canvas, 209½ × 283½ inches
(532 × 720 cm)

Following advice from his teacher
Jacques Louis David, Gros left Paris
for Italy in 1792. Through Josephine
Beauharnais, Gros was introduced to
the young General Bonaparte in
Milan. Gros became Napoleon's official battle painter, and subsequently a
willing glorifier of the new Emperor.
He owed his popularity to his ability
to represent a scene strikingly, yet he
was also the first painter to portray
war from a humanitarian viewpoint
and to show the unspectacular side to
battles and campaigns. To celebrate
Napoleon's victories and expeditions,
Gros painted immense canvases in
which he relinquished the classical
discipline of David in favor of a more
dramatically inspired painting of bril-
liant color.

Helmingham Dell, 1800
Constable, John, 1776–1837
Oil on canvas, 40½ × 50¾ inches
(103 × 129 cm)

While his parents envisaged for Constable a career as a portrait painter, he remained true to his profound love of nature. He did not venture far for his scenes, restricting himself in the main to the Suffolk countryside and the area around Hampstead. Greatly admired in France, especially by the young Romantics, Constable's best-known painting *The Hay Wain* so impressed Delacroix that under its influence he immediately repainted sections of his own *Massacre of Scio*. Constable worked directly from nature, beginning with a drawing or watercolor which served to establish the principle color harmonies and composition. On his return to the studio, these preliminary studies would be worked up into completed paintings.

The Water Garden at Versailles, c.1820
Bonington, Richard Parkes (1802-1828)
Oil on canvas, 28½ × 32½ inches (73 × 83 cm)

Bonington was a master of watercolor and small paintings: his friend and admirer Delacroix said of him, 'You are a king in your own field.' Although English by birth, Bonington trained and worked in France and is said to have rediscovered for the French the lost art of landscape painting, which had been scorned by the followers of David in their pursuit of the antique.

Bonington's *The Water Garden at Versailles* has often mistakenly been called a sketch. Bonington never gave a detailed and smooth finish to his works, preferring to paint rapidly from his impressions. Here, the clothes of the passers-by bring out the tonal values of the large expanse of stormy sky which occupies the greater part of the composition.

The Raft of the Medusa, 1819
Géricault, Théodore, 1791–1824
Oil on canvas, 193 × 282 inches
(491 × 716 cm)

For his Salon submission painting Géricault chose a dramatic scene: the wreck of the frigate *Medusa*, which had set off with a French fleet on an expedition to Senegal but had been lost in July 1816. The French admiralty was accused of having assigned an incompetent officer to lead the expedition; he was the Comte de Chaumareix, a former emigré who had not commanded a ship in more than 25 years. The most horrifying part of the tale recounted by the ten survivors (out of 149 on board the *Medusa*) was being abandoned on a raft with only some casks of wine to sustain them. Drunkenness no doubt aggravated the ensuing abominations. The raft was eventually rescued by the frigate *Argus* after many days adrift. Only fifteen were alive on the raft, five of whom died after being brought ashore. Géricault here concentrates on the last episode; the sighting of the *Argus* by the survivors on the raft. In order to make accurate anatomical studies and to study the behavior of the dying, Géricault worked from a studio conveniently located opposite the Beaujon hospital.

The picture was an enormous success, but mainly on account of the scandal whose flames it fanned. While Géricault received a gold medal, the painting was not purchased by the state and he decided to exhibit it in London and Dublin, where a pamphlet had been published on the wreck of the *Medusa*. In compensation for the lack of a sale, Géricault received a third of the admissions takings – something in the region of 200,000 francs. It seems that the British art public not only had a taste for horror but were also interested in any French catastrophes!

The Death of Sardanapalus,
1826–27
Delacroix, Eugène, 1798–1863
Oil on canvas, 153 × 195 inches
(392 × 496 cm)

For this painting, Delacroix took his theme from a poem by Lord Byron. According to legend, Sardanapalus, an Assyrian ruler, was beseiged in his capital. With no chance of escape he ordered that all his treasures be brought before him – his wives, concubines, servants and horses – and killed and burnt on a vast funeral pyre before killing himself. Delacroix later referred to this painting as his 'massacre number 2', the first being the *Massacre at Scios* from 1824.

Receiving a lukewarm reception at the Salon of 1827, Delacroix nevertheless outraged the Poussinistes of the Neoclassical school with his Rubeniste-inspired work. Support for the painting came from the writer Victor Hugo, whose only regret was that Delacroix had not shown the actual funeral pyre burning. On the other hand, the Director of the Ecole des Beaux-Arts, La Rochefoucauld, who had praised Delacroix in his early days, declared that if that was how he intended to paint, Delacroix could expect no further commissions from him.

The Barque of Dante and Virgil,
1822
Delacroix, Eugène, 1798–1863
Oil on canvas, 74 × 94⅞ inches
(188 × 241 cm)

As well as being a disciple of Théodore Géricault, Delacroix was also greatly influenced by English painters, in particular Bonnington and Fielding. Delacroix was rapidly adopted by the so-called Rubeniste painters, who were grouping together in opposition to the pupils of J L David, the Poussinistes. Delacroix and his friends rebelled against the meticulous draftsmanship and detail of David and Ingres in favor of more vivid color and broader, more open brushwork in the manner of their artistic mentors, Rubens, Hals, Velásquez and Goya. This painting has as its subject a passage from the *Inferno*, the first section of Dante's *Divine Comedy*. In Hell, the Florentine poet's guide is the Roman poet Virgil, who points out the various realms of Hell and the lost souls contained there. In one circle of Hell, souls are condemned to swim eternally in stormy seas.

Instead of the traditional journey to Rome, Delacroix undertook a voyage to the East. In place of the classics of antiquity, the poets of earlier and later romanticism – Dante, Shakespeare, Byron and Goethe – were to be the sources for his work.

Left
Watches, French, nineteenth century

This magnificent display of watches is just a small sample of the treasures of the Louvre. Made in France in the nineteenth century, these watches served not only a functional but also a decorative purpose, a tribute to the ingenuity and skill of the craftsmen who made them. In some instances the shape of the watches belies their timekeeping function: there is one in the shape of a mandolin, another takes the form of a cockle shell made in gold with red enamel and seed pearls. Others are decorated in enamel with fruit or baskets of doves or butterflies. One watch (center top) in the form of an elaborate gold, enamel and pearl pendant also carries its key.

Above
The Turkish Bath, 1862
Ingres, Jean-Auguste-Dominique, 1780-1867
Oil on canvas, 42½ inches diameter (108 cm)

Ingres, David's greatest pupil, lived in Rome for 20 years, ultimately becoming director of the French Academy there. His classical style was largely inspired by Raphael, but for his subject matter he often turned to Romantic sources. The female nude was a subject that interested Ingres all his life. *The Turkish Bath* was the last of his many variations on the theme and displays, as do other works like *The Grande Odalisque* (1814), the fascination with the exotic and oriental that prevailed throughout the nineteenth century. Here, however, the oriental associations of the title are only an excuse for Ingres' variation on the theme of the female nude. Ingres was not interested in anatomy; he changed the shape of the female body to recreate it in idealized forms. It is possible therefore to see him as a forerunner of abstraction, the precursor of artists such as Modigliani and even Picasso.

Right
Souvenir of Marissel, 1850
Corot, Jean-Baptiste-Camille,
1796–1875
Oil on canvas, 21⅝ × 16⅞ inches
(55 × 43 cm)

Although he had not attended the
official studios, Corot, a pupil of the
Neoclassical landscape painters
Michelon and Bertin, followed
French tradition in believing that only
in Italy could he complete his educa-
tion as a landscape painter. Once in
Italy, instead of copying classical
works, Corot devoted his time to
studies of nature, constantly seeking
new motifs and lighting effects. In the
last third of his life, under the influence of the poetry of Virgil, Corot
began to paint woodland scenes and
although his previous paintings had
largely been ignored, these delicate
landscapes made on his annual tours
of the French countryside won him
widespread poularity and acclaim.

Above
Madame Rivière, 1805
Ingres, Jean-Auguste-Dominique,
1780–1867
Oil on canvas, 45¼ × 35⅛ inches
(116 × 90 cm)

Ingres studied with J L David at the
turn of the century and won the Prix
de Rome in 1801, but state finances
were in such a poor way that he was
unable to travel to Rome until 1806.
Meanwhile he remained in Paris and
worked on a number of portraits of
prominent men and their families, including a portrait of Napoleon as First
Consul. Exhibited at the Salon in
Paris in 1806 were three portraits of
the Rivière family: Philibert Rivière,
his wife Madame Rivière and their
daughter. In all these Ingres stressed
the sinuous line forming a silhouette
that both contained and explained the
form.
   While all these portraits revealed
Ingres' ability to convey the individual quality of a face, the paintings
were strongly criticized by the press
and public alike, to the extent that
Ingres vowed not to return to Paris
until he had achieved a major success
in Rome.

Index

Figures in *italics* indicate illustrations

Acknowledgments

The publisher would like to thank David Eldred who designed this book, Helen Jarvis who indexed it, and Liz Montgomery for picture research.
All illustrative material is from the Musée du Louvre, courtesy of the Réunion des musées nationaux, except for the following:
Bettmann Archive: pages 6, 10, 16, 17, 18 (top)
Dr Sally Jeffery: pages 1, 9, 11, 12, 19
UPI/Bettmann: page 18 (bottom)